A Primer of Economic Development

A PRIMER
OF ECONOMIC
DEVELOPMENT

by Robert J. Alexander

THE MACMILLAN COMPANY

A Division of The Crowell-Collier Publishing Company

NEW YORK 1962

*First Printing
The Macmillan Company, New York
Brett-Macmillan Ltd., Galt, Ontario
Printed in the United States of America*

Library of Congress catalog card number: 62-17814

To Mary and Jack Carman

AND THEIR GRANDMOTHERS

Contents

viii

It has always seemed best to me that an author state in advance the point of view from which he intends to discuss his subject. Hence I hasten to do so with regard to the problem of the economic development of the underdeveloped countries. The preconceptions of the present book are two in number, and quite simple. First, I believe in the virtue of democracy as opposed to totalitarianism, for underdeveloped countries as well as for industrialized ones. Second, I believe in the intrinsic value of raising the standards of living of the people of the unindustrialized areas of the globe.

Democracy—by which I mean the right of the governed to select their governors in an orderly manner, and the freedoms of speech, press, thought, and action associated with this right—is essential for the fullest development of the capabilities and spirit of the individual. This development should be, but frequently is not, the objective of organized society.

Democracy is not just something that is good for western Europe and the United States. There is no such thing as a people that is not fit for democracy. There are peoples that have much to learn about the rules to be followed in order to make democracy effective, but there is none for whom democracy is "too good." Hence, I believe that the freedoms and rights associated with democracy are as much to be desired for the peoples of Asia, Africa, and Latin America as for those of western Europe and North America.

Although I should be the first to agree that the societies of western Europe and North America are not the best that can be achieved, I do believe that they offer considerable material advantages over those of the underdeveloped areas. I believe that a people that is well fed, lives in decent homes, and has a high level of education is more likely to be happy and reasonably contented than one that has none of these things. The belief in the "noble savage" is largely confined to those who have never been savages. The glorification of the kind of poverty, misery, and ignorance that exists in the majority of the underdeveloped countries is done largely by those who have never lived under or even seen these conditions.

Believing all this, I have therefore written this book from the point of view of one who believes in the economic development of the underdeveloped countries. I believe that economic development is not only the surest means of providing for the material advancement of the people of the underdeveloped nations but that it is also the most certain means of providing for the ultimate triumph of democracy in those countries. An economy in which prosperity is widely distributed is more conducive to the development of the tolerance and wide agreement on fundamental principles that underlie democracy than is one that is characterized by great extremes of poverty and wealth and a generally inadequate total income. Finally, a relatively high and rising standard of living is more likely to spur the growth or revival of cultural and spiritual values than are filth, poverty, disease, and undernourishment.

The present volume does not pretend to be a definitive or exhaustive study of problems of economic development. Such a book will probably never be written. However, for some time I have felt the need for a relatively short book that would bring together all the principal aspects and problems of economic development in terms a layman would understand. I hope that some economists interested in the problem may find this book worth reading—and perhaps even worth using in their classes on the subject. However, this book is intended primarily for the general reader who has heard some talk and seen many headlines concerning economic development and who may understand the broad concept but wishes to learn more of the particulars.

Economists may find it trying to be told what the law of comparative advantage (or some other basic concept of economic theory) is, but I have hoped that thumbnail summaries of such concepts might help the lay reader to a fuller understanding. I hope that such rudimentary explanations will not discourage too many of my colleagues from reading the pages that follow.

I have tried not only to explain what is meant by economic development but also to indicate why it is so much desired by the people of the underdeveloped countries. Similarly, I have thought not only to picture the principal problems involved in the process of development but also to point out and briefly explain the reasons for the attitudes of the peoples of the developing nations toward these problems. Finally I have dealt with the stake that I feel the more highly developed nations have in the rapid growth of the economies of the other two-thirds of the world.

In an attempt to make this book as readable as possible, I have reduced the footnotes to a minimum, have all but eliminated quotations, and have included only one table. However, I should not want anyone to think that I am attempting to maintain that all the ideas contained herein are original with me, or indeed that any of them are. At various points I have indicated my indebtedness to different authors, and at the end of the book there is a Bibliographical Note to indicate some of the other intellectual borrowings that have gone into the present book.

If there is anything that is in any way new in the present volume, it is perhaps the discussion of the importance of labor problems and the roles trade unionism and social legislation have played in the development of the presently underdeveloped nations. The discussion of the role of the entrepreneur is perhaps posed in a somewhat different manner from that generally used in books on economic development, though I have borrowed heavily there from Schumpeterian concepts. I owe a particular debt of gratitude to Dr. Paul Medow, of the Economics Department of Rutgers University, for introducing me to this approach to the problems of economic development, though, of course, the responsibility for the way it is used here is entirely mine.

This volume is the result not only of reading a good deal in the field but also of considerable personal observation of economic development in a particular area, Latin America.

For more than fifteen years I have been traveling as frequently as my time and finances would allow to that part of the world. Beginning with a major interest in labor problems in the region, I found that my researches soon spread into related problems of politics and economics. One cannot look at any aspect of Latin America these days without soon becoming aware of the tremendous impetus that economic development has, and its effects on the political, social, and even cultural life of these countries.

As a result of my contacts with Latin America, many of the examples I use in this volume are drawn from that area. Perhaps people who know better other underdeveloped areas of the world will feel that I have drawn too many generalizations from the Latin American experience. However, I hope that I have not done so too often and thereby destroyed the value of the book.

As is true with most authors, I owe debts of gratitude for help in bringing this book to completion. Of some of these debts I am probably not myself aware. However, among those of which I am conscious, I wish to mention particularly Professor Alfred P. Thorne, of the University of Puerto Rico, my colleague during the summers of 1958 and 1959, who was patient enough to listen to me expound various ideas in the process of putting them on paper even when, as often occurred, I interrupted some work that he was doing. Dr. Thorne also was kind enough to read the manuscript when it was finished and to make suggestions for its improvement.

I want also to thank my mother, Mrs. R. S. Alexander, and Mrs. J. B. Carman, who read the manuscript from the layman's point of view and suggested a number of changes that make the work more understandable. Others who read it and offered valuable criticisms were Dr. Kenneth Kurihara, Dr. Max

Gideonse, and Dr. Paul Medow, all of the Department of Economics of Rutgers University. Finally, my thanks to my wife, Joan, who not only has borne patiently endless conversations about economic development but who has herself offered valuable insights and suggestions drawn from her own observations of the process of economic development on the spot in Latin America.

R. J. A.

Rutgers University
New Brunswick, New Jersey
January 1962

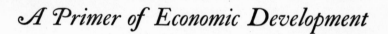

A Primer of Economic Development

1

What Do We Mean by Underdevelopment and Economic Development?

The world today is divided into rich countries and poor countries. This fact is well known and understood in the poor countries, and it is pressing itself more and more upon the attention of the peoples of the rich ones. It is one of the great issues of the politics, economics, and international relations of the second half of the twentieth century. Basically, this division of the world, its consequences, and attempts to do something about narrowing the differences between the rich countries on the one hand and the poor ones on the other, is the theme of this book.

The peoples of the poor countries make up two-thirds of the world's population. Most of them are now established in independent, sovereign nations, and the rest will certainly achieve this status within the next few years. They already constitute the great majority of the votes in the United Nations, and though they are militarily weak, their force of numbers continues to grow apace, and the unrest that characterizes these countries cannot help being a disturbing factor in world politics. Moreover, if conditions do not change, explosions in these countries can only be postponed; they cannot be avoided completely.

The peoples of the rich nations are not entirely unaware of these facts. The problem of economic development of the underdeveloped countries has become a favorite topic of conversation since World War II. This is not surprising. Finley Peter Dunne once had the fabulous Mr. Dooley comment that "The Supreme Court follows the election returns." In the same way, the economists, the politicians, and the newspapers follow in the wake of events, and are especially concerned with the problems that are most pressing at any given moment.

Thus, during the 1930's the economists and the politicians concentrated their attention on ways and means of overcoming the business cycle, because the Depression was the world's most pressing economic problem at that time. In the same way, since World War II economic development has become a matter of wide interest and heated discussion because it is one of the most crucial problems of the postwar world.

The fact is that there is in progress today what the Swedish economist Gunnar Myrdal has called the Great Awakening in the so-called "underdeveloped" countries. It is as if the people who constitute two-thirds of the world's population had awakened from a long sleep and, like Rip Van Winkle, had suddenly become aware that the world around them had changed. They are frantically engaged in trying to catch up with this change.

As a result, the nations with underdeveloped economies are becoming increasingly critical of the economically more advanced countries. Rightly or wrongly, they blame the more advanced nations for all or part of their own lack of development. At the same time, they turn to the more advanced countries for aid in their own process of growth.

DEVELOPED AND UNDERDEVELOPED COUNTRIES

What do we mean by the underdeveloped countries? What do we mean by the developed countries? These are not such simple questions, at least to the economists, as they appear to be at first glance. One of the favorite indoor sports of economists who are interested in this problem is to classify the nations of the world as "developed" and "underdeveloped." Some economists would add a third category, "partly developed." Considerable confusion results from all of this.

However, in general terms it is not too difficult to differentiate between the two groups of nations. Thus, the countries of northwestern Europe, plus the United States and Canada, are the highly developed, advanced, industrial nations. On the other hand, the countries of Latin America, Africa, non-Communist Asia (with the exception of Japan), and of Communist Asia, too, for that matter, though we are not particularly concerned with them in the present volume, are the underdeveloped, unindustrialized, "backward" nations.

Some economists object to the terms "developed" and "underdeveloped" to describe the two groups of countries of which we are talking. They point out that the so-called "developed" nations have by no means ceased their economic growth and that indeed they tend to grow even more rapidly than the so-called "underdeveloped" ones. However, since one has to use some kind of category to differentiate between the two groups of countries, and one group is in all regards more advanced economically than the other, we may be content to use these terms, in spite of the qualms of the purists. It is also convenient, for the sake of variety, to use from time to time the terms "less advanced" and "developing" instead of "underdeveloped" to categorize those countries that are the subject of this book—and we shall use these terms.

Certainly there is no intention of indicating inherent inferiority in using the word "underdeveloped." Many of the countries that are in this stage at the present time are nations with long and glorious histories. Civilizations flourished in India, China, Iraq, and Iran when the ancestors of the present Europeans or North Americans were dressed in animal skins and living in caves. However, these countries over the course of centuries have fallen behind the countries of western Europe and the northern half of the Western Hemisphere in terms of material progress. Until recently, the Industrial Revolution and all its economic, social, and political effects had passed them by. Only now are they beginning to "catch up" with the younger civilizations of the industrialized countries.

When the problem of economic development first became popular, use was made of the word "backward" to describe the nations that had fallen behind in the economic race. However, there was considerable protest from statesmen, economists, political leaders, and scholars in these countries, and since World War II the term "backward" has given way to "underdeveloped," which in any case is more descriptive.

Even those economists who have no hesitation in talking about the economically "underdeveloped" and the "developed" nations frequently cannot agree on just which nation belongs in which category. It is not difficult to decide which countries are at the extremes. Few people would quarrel with the proposition that the United States, West Germany, Great Britain, the Scandinavian countries, Switzerland, the Low Countries, and France are "developed." Nor would anyone raise much objection to putting Ghana and Nigeria in West Africa, Burma and Indonesia in Asia, or Honduras and Paraguay in Latin America in the "underdeveloped" category.

The difficulties arise when one looks at those countries that have a relatively high standard of living but that in one way or another have lopsided economies, exceedingly subject to changes brought about by fluctuations in the international market place over which they have little or no control. For example, Argentina, Australia, and New Zealand are countries that enjoy standards of living better than those of perhaps 85 per cent of the other nations of the world. Yet they may correctly be considered as "underdeveloped." *

CRITERIA OF UNDERDEVELOPMENT

In order to clarify the issue, it is well to set forth a set of criteria to define "underdevelopment." To our mind, there are seven basic qualities underdeveloped nations possess. All underdeveloped countries do not have all of them but all under-

---

* Some readers may be seeking a precise listing of just which countries in the world are underdeveloped, and how much so. However, we have preferred not to make such a listing. No matter how many categories of underdeveloped nations one might establish, and which countries were placed in which category, it would be impossible to satisfy everyone. We have felt it more advisable to state in general terms which countries are in the underdeveloped category, and then to specify the characteristics we consider qualify a nation for being placed in that category. Each reader is free to decide for himself whether he cares to place country X or country Y in the list. The responsibility is then his, not the author's.

developed countries do have one or more of them. These qualities are: (1) a low per capita real income; (2) an "unbalanced" economy; (3) natural resources that are either largely untapped or are being used by and for the benefit of the highly industrialized nations; (4) a tradition-oriented rather than a market-oriented economy; (5) small amounts of capital equipment relative to the labor force; (6) structural underemployment; and (7) the widespread belief among the people of the country that it is "underdeveloped."

Certainly the great majority of the underdeveloped nations have very low per capita incomes. The real income of the average citizen of the United States is ten to one hundred times that of the average resident of India, Ghana, Haiti, or Indonesia. The people of many though not all of the underdeveloped nations have incomes that are so low that they have enough to eat only in very good years, and a flood, a drought, or some other natural disaster can cause widespread starvation. Even in good times these people suffer from malnutrition, and know nothing of most of the goods that people in the United States and western Europe consider "necessities." Low per capita income, which is perhaps the most important single characteristic of underdevelopment, would by itself classify most African nations, the vast majority of Asian ones, and the majority of the Latin American countries as "underdeveloped."

Also characteristic of underdeveloped countries, even of those with relatively high per capita income and standards of living, is the phenomenon of an "unbalanced" economy. By this we mean an economy that depends very heavily on the exportation of raw materials or foodstuffs; that exports only one such item or at most a very narrow range of unprocessed agricultural or mineral products. These economies, as we shall demonstrate in a later chapter, are subject to violent fluctuations and are at the mercy of markets they cannot control, and their prosperity or lack of it is a mere reflection of that of the highly industrialized nations. So long as they remain underdeveloped, they have no way of protecting themselves against this situation. At the same time these countries produce a relatively small part of the consumers' goods their populations need, and they have to depend on importing these from abroad.

Objection may be made that some of the western European industrial countries are as dependent on exports as are the countries we have generally classed as underdeveloped, or even more so. Great Britain, Belgium, and the Netherlands might be mentioned. However, there are several fundamental differences between the positions of these countries and those of the underdeveloped nations. For one thing, the western European nations are exporting a wide variety of industrial goods, in addition to providing an almost equally wide variety of services to the rest of the world. They do not therefore depend excessively on one or two products, as do most of the underdeveloped nations. In the second place, as large importers of raw materials and foodstuffs they have an influence in international markets that is not matched by that of any underdeveloped country. They thus have a considerable degree of "monopsony"—that is, of control over the products they buy. They also have a certain degree of monopoly—control over the products they sell—since the principal producers are large companies that have a definite influence in the market in which they are selling, and most of them participate in cartel arrangements as well, whereby markets are partitioned to some degree among all available suppliers. Finally, they produce such a variety of things for their own market that the

7

decline of one export is not going to leave the country without sufficient resources to obtain food, consumers' goods, or other vital things their consumers need, as is the case with many of the underdeveloped nations.

The very phrase "underdeveloped" means that the natural resources of these countries are not being used to the extent that they might be. They have resources that lie dormant because the economy of the country does not have at present any way in which to use them. Or, in some cases, some of their minerals or their petroleum or their agricultural products may have been developed by foreign firms for shipment to foreign countries only. In other words, the raw materials of these countries have not been developed for the use of their own economies.

Some economists criticize this description of an underdeveloped nation on the grounds that the highly industrialized nations also have resources that they have not developed. This may be true, but in those cases it is due to one of two peculiar circumstances. Either the industrialized country finds that it can obtain those resources more cheaply abroad, and therefore does not develop its own high-cost raw materials, or no use has yet been discovered for these resources.

The United States presents instances of both of these phenomena. It certainly possesses resources of copper, of low-grade iron, of oil, or other minerals that are not being mined because it is cheaper to obtain higher-grade, less costly materials from Chile or Venezuela or Labrador. Furthermore, the United States possessed for many decades reserves of uranium, for which there was little or no use until the advent of the Atomic Age, and undoubtedly has other resources for which there is still no use.

However, these facts do not reduce the state of economic

development of the United States. When the United States finds it convenient for its own economy to develop its own resources it does so; it does not have to wait for some more highly industrialized power to open up these raw materials for its own use, regardless of the nation's needs or economy.

Many of the underdeveloped nations are custom-dominated. Economic as well as social relations are determined by tradition, and the market plays little part. Production is on a local basis for local needs rather than for sale in an impersonal general market. The means of production, principally the land, are in the hands of vested groups who use them in ways that have been customary since time immemorial and who have little incentive or interest in introducing innovations or in new ways of doing things.

One key aspect of underdevelopment is the fact that countries in this stage have a low ratio between capital goods and the labor force. Machinery and other capital equipment are relatively scarce, and there is a great deal more dependence on human and animal muscles than there is in the more highly developed nations. As we shall see, one of the basic problems of the underdeveloped countries as they undertake the process of development is the accumulation of a stock of machinery and other capital goods.

Underemployment is almost synonymous with underdevelopment. In virtually all the less advanced nations there are large numbers of people, particularly in agriculture, but also in commerce and in the shops of the artisans, who are not fully employed. Their capacities are being only partially used, or they are being wasted on some activity that contributes little to the total product of the nation. Agriculture is usually overstaffed; the petty vendor hawks his wares on the street, selling little at the cost of considerable time and effort; the small craftsman has in his employ excess members of his family or the families of his friends who could not get employment elsewhere. This factor is an advantage in some instances, when the process of development gets under way. Then underemployment makes it possible to draw people out of current activities in which too many workers are employed into new ones arising out of economic development, without any lessening in the total output of the economy.

Finally, an important consideration in classifying countries in the underdeveloped category is the way in which their inhabitants regard themselves. Thus the Argentines, though their country has one of the world's highest standards of living, regard their nation as "underdeveloped," and feel a bond of kinship with other underdeveloped areas of the world. One might also add that their economy is still considerably "unbalanced," in the sense that we have used this term, and that capital equipment is still relatively scarce in comparison with that of the highly industrialized nations.

LIMITS OF DEVELOPMENT

Of course, all countries cannot develop equally. This is a point made by some economists in the highly industrialized nations. They maintain that all the commotion over the problems of economic growth of the underdeveloped nations is a tempest in a teapot. They usually add that if these countries had the capacity to develop and to industrialize they would do so "naturally," if one would only trust to the forces of the market and of international trade, which would "automatically" bring about the development of the resources of all countries of the world when and if they are "needed."

Though clear-thinking people in the underdeveloped nations would be the first to admit the general proposition stated, they would not draw the same conclusions from it. It is obvious that Costa Rica, a country of less than one million people, is never going to have the complex kind of economy the United States possesses. Indeed, only a few other nations will ever reach the degree of development the leading industrial powers possess.

However, there is a widespread feeling in the underdeveloped countries that every effort should be made so that each country can grow to the limits of its capacity. Countries that can quite reasonably have textile industries, packing houses, shoe factories, grain mills, sugar refineries, and so on, should not be forever content to have only agriculture and to allow the large industrial countries to produce and ship to them all of their consumers' goods.

On the other hand, there is undoubtedly a handful of the presently underdeveloped nations that in time may well equal or surpass the present highly industrialized nations. They have the resources, the population, the potential talent to make this a possibility. Furthermore, the peoples of these nations see no reason why they should remain for generations the international hewers of wood and drawers of water, or why they should not develop their nations as rapidly as possible and bring into being the complex economies they are capable of maintaining.

Some people in the highly industrialized countries feel that economic development (and particularly industrialization) are in themselves bad. These are the believers in the "noble savage" who argue that the agricultural and the pastoral life have infinite charms that are lost when industrialization begins. They praise the virtues of the "simple peasant," and see only disaster in his conversion into a factory worker. These people

11

are generally professors or economists who have incomes that in most of the underdeveloped nations would be regarded as fabulous, who live in comfortable houses in a big or medium-sized city, have a car and at least their share of the "gadgets" of an industrial society which they so much deplore. The people of the underdeveloped nations find it hard to take them seriously.

The fact is that life in the underdeveloped countries is not so idyllic as some would have us think. There is dense poverty there; people have insufficient food, one change of clothing, and live in primitive houses. They swelter in the summer and freeze in the winter; they see their children die of undernourishment, and until recently saw others perish of epidemic diseases. They have little recreation, even less education, and are often oppressed socially, economically, and politically.

URGENCY OF ECONOMIC DEVELOPMENT

Of course, in most of these nations such conditions have existed for centuries, perhaps for millenniums. It has been argued that throughout history the peoples of the underdeveloped nations have been happy in spite of poverty, filth, and disease and that they are better left as they are. However, the significant fact is that the peoples of the underdeveloped nations are no longer willing to remain as they are.

The impact of several centuries of contact with the countries of western Europe and the growing awareness that it is possible to live differently have aroused a profound desire in great masses of the people in the underdeveloped nations to change the whole pattern of their existence. Whether they are right or wrong, they feel that they can be happier if they can partake of some of the material prosperity that the coun-

12

tries of western Europe and North America have enjoyed. They feel a desire not only for material improvement but also for cultural and spiritual development. They yearn for education, for greater contact with the outside world; they want to learn from the countries of the West.

This desire for change was first felt in the years before and during World War I among the intellectuals of many of the underdeveloped nations. Between the world wars it slowly penetrated deeper into the masses. This was a yearning not only for material improvement but also for social change and national self-expression. These ideas had come largely from the highly industrialized nations themselves, though the influence of the Russian Revolution—and particularly its example of how a formerly underdeveloped nation can industrialize rapidly—should not be underestimated.

The peoples of the underdeveloped countries have assimilated well all these lessons. The movement for economic development, which is part of a much broader pattern of social and political and economic change in the underdeveloped nations, had by the end of World War II enlisted the support of wide elements of the masses in virtually all the underdeveloped nations. Since then it has taken the shape of positive attempts by the peoples and governments of one underdeveloped country after another to spur the process of economic diversification and industrialization.

The objectives of this "crusade" for economic development are ones that men of good will everywhere can accept. Economic growth is sought as a means of raising standards of living of the peoples in these countries. It is pursued as a way of making it possible to raise the cultural levels of the vast masses who are illiterate, superstitious, and in some cases primitive. It is pushed for the purpose of establishing a strong basis for the national life of many new nations, and many old ones as well that have until recently had little real national consciousness. Finally, economic development is sought by the leaders of many of the underdeveloped nations as a solid base for the development of the kind of political democracy many of these leaders themselves have learned about and come to appreciate in the highly industrialized nations of western Europe and North America.

It is worth noting that the objectives of the developing countries in the non-Communist world differ considerably from those on the other side of the Iron and Bamboo curtains. In the Communist countries the emphasis is on national power, military might, and the establishment of a firm base for the ultimate conquest of the rest of the world for Communism. Standards of living and other benefits for the masses of the people will be and are being sacrificed to these objectives—as both Soviet Russia and Communist China bear witness.

The movement for economic development can no longer be suppressed—if it ever could. It is a major force in the world. It finds echo in the United Nations and in all its specialized agencies. It is a fundamental fact of politics in virtually all the underdeveloped countries. Economic development is the issue that nations representing two-thirds of the non-Communist world feel to be the most pressing problem on the globe today.

The people of the highly developed countries can overlook or pretend not to see this problem only at their own peril. The underdeveloped nations have determined to make their economies grow and diversify as rapidly as possible. The road they have chosen for themselves is a hard one, full of pitfalls and difficulties. They will undoubtedly make many mistakes; there will be many failures along the way. But of one thing we can be sure—the underdeveloped nations will continue, for the next few generations at least, to try to achieve their goal.

It would be frivolous and dangerous indeed for the peoples of western Europe and of the United States to be unaware of what is going on in the rest of the non-Communist world. We hope that from the pages that follow it will be possible to draw enlightenment concerning the reasons that impel the less advanced countries to try to develop, as well as some of the difficulties they are encountering and are likely to encounter, some of the policies they are following, and the possible role the already industrialized nations may be able to play in this process.

2

Why Do They Want Economic Development?

Why do the peoples of the "underdeveloped" countries want economic development? Why has industrialization become a plank in the platform of virtually all political parties in these countries, and part of the program of nearly every government in the nonindustrial nations? The answers to these questions are complex. Some of them are economic; others might better be called political.

DANGERS OF MONOPRODUCT ECONOMIES

The first reason for industrialization is the fact that the people of the underdeveloped countries are well aware of the dangers inherent in unbalanced or "monoproduct" economies

—economies that depend on one or a small number of export products for all their foreign-exchange income. There is a widespread desire to develop more balanced economies.

Virtually all underdeveloped nations are producers of foodstuffs or agricultural or mineral raw materials. They grow coffee, cocoa, or sugar, or produce copper, tin, or gold, for example. Most of these nations produce only a few such products, and they produce them for export, not principally for use within their frontiers. With the income they earn abroad by selling these raw materials and foodstuffs, they purchase the manufactured goods needed by the populace, and sometimes import sizable amounts of processed foodstuffs as well.

The degree to which some of the underdeveloped nations are dependent on their principal exports is shown by the table on page 19.

This kind of economy is highly unstable, and vulnerable to external changes. Prices of raw materials and foodstuffs change frequently and violently for reasons completely outside the control of the producers. A slight drop in the demand in the United States or western Europe for coffee, for instance, can have catastrophic effects on the economy of a country that has little else to export. A small drop in price can spell disaster for the nation's whole economy. Thus, for example, a reduction of $0.01 in the price of tin, upon which Bolivia is almost solely dependent for its foreign exchange, results in a fall of $600,000 to $700,000 in the national income of that country.* It brings unemployment and reduced income to the segment of the economy that often is the biggest and frequently the

* Victor Paz Estenssoro, "Mensaje del Presidente de la República al Honorable Congreso" (Imprenta Nacional, La Paz, Bolivia, 1956), p. 18.

best-paying employer. Both the export and the import trade suffer. Furthermore, deprived of sizable amounts of foreign exchange, the country is unable to import necessary consumers' goods.

Table One

DEPENDENCE OF UNDERDEVELOPED COUNTRIES ON PRINCIPAL EXPORTS *

Country	Commodity	Year	% of Foreign Exchange from Principal Export
Bolivia	Tin	1956	54.9
Brazil	Coffee	1956	69.5
Burma	Rice	1955	74.7
Chile	Copper	1955	70.3
Ghana	Cocoa	1956	66.3
Iraq	Petroleum	1956	92.2
Liberia	Rubber	1956	67.9
Malaya	Rubber	1956	51.5

* Compiled from United Nations *Yearbook of International Trade Statistics*, 1956, Vol. I.

Many economically advanced nations have recognized the dangers of the fluctuations of production and prices of raw materials and foodstuffs within their own borders. Thus the United States has developed an elaborate program for guaranteeing minimum prices to its farmers, and many other nations have done likewise. But the underdeveloped nations enjoy little such assurance of stable production and income in the international market.

19

The underdeveloped country is usually unable to exercise any extensive control over the sale and price of its principal export product. The futile attempts by Brazil over a period of fifty years to control the price of coffee—the net result of which was to encourage a dozen other Latin American countries to develop their coffee industries—are witness of this fact.

The demand for the products of the underdeveloped nations is determined by the needs of the industrialized nations. The prosperity of the manufacturing nations of Europe and North America results in prosperity for the countries producing the raw materials and foods needed by those nations. A decline in economic activity in the industrial nations is immediately reflected in an even greater decline in the nations in the "periphery," the underdeveloped countries. However, the reverse is not true—the state of economic health of the underdeveloped countries has relatively little impact on that of the highly developed parts of the world.

Even very high prices for raw materials and foodstuffs can bring disaster for an underdeveloped nation that depends solely on a limited range of these for its foreign-exchange income. High prices may induce a relatively sudden increase in output, which shortly thereafter will have a catastrophic effect by inducing overproduction and low prices. Thus, the high price of coffee in the late 1940's encouraged Brazilian farmers greatly to expand plantings of coffee trees, with the result that by the middle 1950's the country had a very large excess of the bean, and prices fell catastrophically.

These sharp and rapid changes in raw material and food prices would not have such bad consequences for the underdeveloped nations if the prices of the manufactured goods they buy in return for their exports varied in the same way. However, they do not. The prices of industrial products are relatively stable, since they are generally produced by large semimonopolistic firms that are able to cut back production in the face of a reduced demand, instead of lowering prices.

Farmers in the United States are well aware of this tendency of industrial prices to stay steady while raw material and food prices vary widely. From their awareness has arisen the demand of the American agriculturalists for "parity," for the assurance to them of a price that will keep agricultural prices in the United States more or less in conformity with the prices of manufactured goods. The people of the underdeveloped countries are demanding similar arrangements on a worldwide scale.

Not only is a nonindustrial country subject to sharp and frequent variations of price for its products; it is also subject to possible disaster if something happens to the principal commodity it ships abroad. If a disease destroys trees or plants bearing this product, a whole economy can be undermined. If technological developments reduce the importance of, and therefore the demand for, a country's export, the same result may follow.

The underdeveloped nations have frequently experienced such disasters. During the first decade of the twentieth century, Brazil was the great exporter of wild natural rubber, and prosperity came to the cities and towns of the Amazon Valley. When the countries of the Far East began to produce plantation rubber, Brazil was unable to compete, and grass grew in the streets of what had once been prosperous centers of population. In Costa Rica, when the Panama disease hit the country's banana plantations, the economy of the whole eastern half of the nation was reduced to the level of poverty and misery.

21

Chile had perhaps the most dramatic experience of this kind. Before World War I that country's principal export was natural nitrates, of which it produced approximately 90 per cent of the world's supply. When Chilean exports to Central Europe were cut off as a result of the war, the Germans invented and put into use a process for extracting nitrogen from the air. Once the world conflict was over, Chile's markets for natural nitrates had been destroyed. For more than a decade the Chilean economy suffered the consequences of this nitrate crisis, which brought not only economic disaster but also political turbulence.

Three events since 1914 have brought home forcefully to the underdeveloped countries the instability and vulnerability of an economy that is too dependent on the export of a limited range of raw materials and foodstuffs. These were the First World War, the Great Depression, and the Second World War.

During World War I the major food- and raw-material-producing nations found themselves cut off not only from the markets for their products but also from their sources of manufactured goods. Although the demand for raw materials and some food products improved after the first months of the war, the underdeveloped countries found themselves unable to obtain many of the manufactured products they needed, so long as the war lasted. They either had to do without these products or find some way of making them themselves.

The Great Depression was even more catastrophic for the underdeveloped nations. As a result of the crisis in the economies of the manufacturing nations, their demand for minerals and agricultural products from the unindustrialized nations dried up. The countries that produced what are sometimes called the "dessert products"—coffee, tea, sugar—found that the demand for their exports dropped precipitately. However, even the producers of commodities used in industrial production, such as copper, oil, tin, found that the reduced output of the manufacturing countries meant a much reduced demand for their products at drastically lower prices. The result was a fall in income and employment for the export industries and for everyone associated with getting those industries' output to market; a fall in income and employment in the import business as well, since without foreign exchange from their export industry these countries could not import the goods they needed. Once again, they either had to go without essential products or somehow produce them themselves.

The story was repeated once again during World War II. Although exports of the principal raw materials and foodstuffs held up well, the underdeveloped countries were unable to receive in return the manufactured goods they required, since the warring Great Powers were concentrating on turning out goods for their war efforts, and had little to spare to supply the needs of the underdeveloped nations.

After World War II the underdeveloped nations encountered an added inconvenience. They had been forced to sell their raw materials and foodstuffs during the war at prices fixed at a low level by the big industrial powers. But after the conflict was over, when the time came for the underdeveloped nations to spend the income they had earned during the war, they found that price controls had been removed in the industrialized nations and that they were forced to pay much higher prices for their imports.

As a result of their experiences as producers of raw materials and foodstuffs, the peoples of the underdeveloped countries have become convinced that they must get away from an excessive dependence upon the production of a few agricultural or mineral commodities. They have become convinced that they must have a more diversified economy that will provide employment and basic consumers' goods whether the demand for their export products is good or bad, whether the major industrial powers are in the grip of a depression or in the midst of a war, or are prosperous and at peace with one another. They feel that they must have at least some manufacturing industry to provide this employment and produce these necessary goods.

FULL USE OF RESOURCES

The dangers inherent in a monoproduct economy are not the only reasons the peoples of the underdeveloped nations are seeking economic development. The peoples of many of these nations have come to realize that they have ample resources for developing manufacturing industry. They wish to put these resources to use for their own benefit.

Brazil, for instance, has vast quantities of iron ore, of copper, bauxite, petroleum, and other important minerals. It produces cotton, sugar, vegetable oils, and wool, all important agricultural raw materials. It has large potential hydroelectric reserves, as well as coal in large amounts, though of poor quality. It has virtually all the raw materials needed by a major industrial power.

Every underdeveloped nation is not by any means so richly endowed as Brazil. But there are few of them that do not have raw-material resources for some industrial enterprise. Even Liberia in West Africa has rubber and iron ore, and could probably grow a wide range of tropical agricultural raw materials. Nigeria, also in West Africa, has bauxite, iron ore, petroleum, and is also a producer of a variety of agricultural

24

commodities. Burma, one of the newly independent Asian nations, has iron, coal, and minerals, and could produce large quantities of cotton, vegetable oils, and other agricultural products essential to industry.

Present production of raw materials is not always an indication of a country's potentialities. Thus, in Colombia a sizable cotton textile industry developed under the impetus of the Great Depression and World War II, although the country produced little cotton. Their need for raw materials induced the textile manufacturers to undertake the establishment of cotton plantations in the rich Cauca Valley. The Colombian Government aided this project, and the country is now rapidly becoming self-sufficient in this important raw material.

In many cases a beginning has been made to utilize the underdeveloped countries' resources. Powerful firms from the industrialized countries have opened up mines or plantations to produce raw materials for the use of the developed nations' industries. They have thus given some indication of the potentialities of the underdeveloped countries' economies. However, the people of the underdeveloped nations are no longer satisfied with such exploitation of their resources for the benefit of their richer and more powerful neighbors. Insofar as possible, they wish to see them used for the benefit of their own economies, and they desire to open up resources that have hitherto gone untapped.

Many of the underdeveloped nations are faced with pressing population problems. As a result of advances in public health services, epidemics of diseases that used to kill off millions of people each year have been brought under control or entirely eradicated. Thus the death rate has dropped sharply in almost all countries during recent decades. However, in the underdeveloped countries birth rates remain extremely high, with the result that populations are increasing with unheard-of rapidity.

Traditional agriculture cannot absorb all this increase in population. The only way in which the increase can be prevented from drastically reducing already pitiably low standards of living is by finding new occupations for the growing numbers of people. This means economic development. Better agricultural methods and larger amounts of land under cultivation must be provided to grow enough food to feed the increased number of mouths. New jobs in industry, in commerce, and in the service trades must be created in order to give work to the large numbers who enter the labor force for the first time each year. The increase in the extent and productivity of agriculture and industrialization and the general diversification of the economy are the essence of economic development.

CONTACTS WITH INDUSTRIAL COUNTRIES

The desire of the peoples of the raw-material and food-producing nations to develop manufacturing industry is strengthened by their increasing contacts with the outside world. Growing trade relations, quicker and more ample transportation facilities, and the propaganda efforts of two world wars and a cold war have all served to make the peoples of the underdeveloped nations more aware of what goes on in the economically more advanced parts of the world. Perhaps the single most important source of knowledge for the common man in the cities of the underdeveloped countries is the motion picture, especially those produced in the United States. Although many films give misleading and one-sided views of life in the more highly developed nations, they nonetheless have a powerful impact.

Two basic conclusions emerge in the minds of the peoples of the underdeveloped countries from their contacts with the industrialized part of the world: that the economically advanced countries are more powerful than the underdeveloped nations, militarily and politically, and that the people in the industrialized nations have much higher standards of living than they themselves possess.

A third conclusion that derives from these other two may or may not be erroneous, but it is very widespread: the reason that the countries of western Europe and the United States are richer and more powerful is that they are industrialized. Hence, the peoples of Asia, Africa, and Latin America are anxious to acquire the manufacturing industries they feel are the key to wealth, power, and a higher standard of living.

IMPACT OF NATIONALISM

Closely associated with this "keeping up with the international Joneses" motivation for development is the growth of modern nationalism in the underdeveloped nations. Since World War II the collapse of the great empires has seen the emergence of several score new nations, jealous of their newly won political sovereignty, and anxious to supplement this by achieving "economic independence" as well. Other underdeveloped nations with a longer history of political independence, such as those of Latin America, have also experienced an intensification of nationalism.

What the nationalist masses of the underdeveloped countries mean by "economic independence" is not always clear. However, its broad outlines can be indicated. The argument runs that a country whose economic life is contingent on the willingness of one or two industrialized nations to buy its main export is in a vulnerable position. It is likely to be subject to a type of pressure from those industrialized countries that will severely limit its political sovereignty. The weaker country can be forced to conform to the desires of the industrialized power under the threat of a refusal to purchase the commodity the underdeveloped nation must sell for its very existence.

This argument is intensified in cases where the firms exploiting the underdeveloped nation's principal export are controlled by citizens of the country to which this export is largely shipped. Internal as well as external pressures can then be brought to bear, it is argued, by the economically more powerful nation upon the weaker one.

The nationalists of the underdeveloped countries believe that the only way in which the political sovereignty of their nations can be given a solid economic base is by greater diversification of economic life, that is, industrialization, and by either severely limiting or by completely abolishing the influence of the foreign firms which produce their nations' main exports. Extreme nationalists go further than this, and seek completely to eliminate foreign firms from all aspects of the economy; but in most countries they are not as yet the majority.

INDUSTRIALIZATION AND SOCIAL CHANGE

Economic development and industrialization are sought not only as means of strengthening the nation but also as means of bringing about a shift of power within the underdeveloped nation. Most of these countries are dominated, or have until recently been dominated, by small aristocracies or oligarchies, the economic and political power of which originated from their possession of most of the nation's arable or cultivated land.

In contrast to them have been the great masses of the rural population, living under some form of servitude or peonage, and extracting a bare subsistence from the soil by antiquated methods and primitive implements and earning little or no money income.

Even before the advent of industrialization on an appreciable scale, groups tended to develop, particularly among the intelligentsia and professional classes, who were opposed to this traditional economic and social pattern. The growth of industry provides these advocates of change with strong allies, and it undermines the position of the oligarchical classes. It brings into existence two economic and social classes whose interests are strongly opposed to those of the rural landholders: the factory owners and managers, and the industrial workers.

The factory owners are anxious to extend the market for their goods. They particularly desire to see the great mass of agricultural workers brought into the market, which means that they must favor the destruction of the traditional pattern in the countryside, which deprives the mass of agriculturalists of money income. The manufacturer also is anxious to get protection for his industry, whereas the landowner is interested in importing his consumer goods at the cheapest price possible.

The industrial worker also has interests in opposition to those of the landholder. The latter will naturally oppose any attempts by urban workers to organize to improve their conditions, in fear that such organization will incite his own workers to establish unions also. Furthermore, the industrial worker shares with his employer the desire to acquire the largest possible markets for the products of their factory, and so will be for a change in the countryside, as well as for protection for manufacturing.

Finally, the growth of manufacturing generally strengthens

the political position of the city as opposed to the landlord-dominated countryside. Sooner or later control of the nation will pass to the more dynamic urban centers, and thus will make it more difficult for the landholders to defend the *status quo*. Hence, all those elements in the nation that favor a reform in rural areas tend to favor the growth of industrialization. The growth of industry becomes a means for achieving social reform.

Thus there are economic, nationalist, social, and political reasons for the widespread desire for economic development in the countries of Africa, Asia, and Latin America. All these arguments are perhaps not of equal weight. Some are more important in one country than in another. Some appeal more to one class or group than they do to another. However, taken together, they present the rationale that explains the almost overpowering yearning of the peoples and governments of the underdeveloped nations to diversify their economies and in particular to establish manufacturing. They explain what is perhaps the most powerful political-economic drive in the world of the mid-twentieth century. These reasons must be understood by the people of the already industrialized countries.

3

Protection of Industry in Developing Countries

Protection of industry is essential for a country that is going through the process of economic development. This simple statement is well understood in the underdeveloped countries. However, it sends shivers down the spines of many economists (and politicians) of the already industrialized nations. These people tend to ignore the histories of their own countries, and to trot out the so-called "Law of Comparative Advantage" as a universal rule, applicable to all times and all places. They feel that it proves that "free trade" is not only the most natural but also the most "scientific" method of conducting international economic relations.

Stated simply, the Law of Comparative Advantage is this: Every nation is best advised to concentrate on the production of those goods experience shows that it can produce most cheaply, exporting its surpluses of those commodities in return for other goods that it could produce only at greater cost. Thus, the Law states, there would be the maximum international division of labor. Since each nation would be producing those things for which it could get the greatest output for the least effort, the total world output would be the greatest possible. Hence consumption would also be the highest possible. Finally, the argument runs that free trade will not impede the development of new industries, including manufacturing, in those countries that do not possess them, because if those countries have a "natural" advantage for such industries this will in time become obvious, and the industries will appear.

The briefest practical answer to the universal claims of the Law of Comparative Advantage is that in the best of all possible worlds the Law might result in the greatest welfare for all nations and all peoples, but that unfortunately we do not live in the best of all possible worlds. The Law of Comparative Advantage might make sense for all countries of the world (1) if there were no wars great and small to cut mineral and agricultural economies off from their markets and from their sources of manufactured goods; (2) if there were no economic depressions originating in industrial nations and being exported to those countries producing raw materials and foodstuffs; (3) if the demand for and price of all commodities moved more or less together, instead of the present situation in which manufactured goods are relatively steady, while prices of raw materials and foodstuffs oscillate rapidly: However, as the globe is organized today, with these conditions not existing, the Law of Comparative Advantage works to the benefit of the great manufacturing nations and to the detriment of the producers of raw materials and foodstuffs—the underdeveloped nations.

There are other arguments, of a more theoretical nature, which also may be offered in reply to the Law of Comparative Advantage. The theory presumes that there exists full employment of all natural resources and labor in all countries. If this were true, it would follow that if a country were to start to produce a new type of commodity it had never made before—let us say, manufactured goods—it would have to divert natural resources and manpower from uses in which they were already fully employed. Such diversion would mean that labor and resources would be transferred from fields where they were relatively productive to those in which their productivity was less.

This description does not fit the facts in the underdeveloped countries. As we have already noted, there exists in most of these countries a considerable reserve of labor that is either unemployed or is partially employed, and could produce a great deal more if it could be used in a field in which it could be completely occupied. At the same time, most underdeveloped nations have extensive natural resources that have gone untapped because it has not as yet served the interests of the highly industrialized countries to try to use them.

The second presupposition of the Law of Comparative Advantage is that there is "full development" as well as full employment throughout the world. This is to say that it is presumed that the full extent of technological development has been reached. This certainly is not the case either in the developed or in the underdeveloped nations. It is true that with the technology hitherto used in the underdeveloped countries, manufacturing has not been practicable. However, the very essence of economic growth and development is the discovery and application of "innovations" or changes in traditional ways of producing and exchanging goods. The introduction of innovations can change the "comparative advantage" of a country very rapidly and very frequently, and can give an underdeveloped nation an advantage it did not have previously. However, in the underdeveloped countries innovations need time to become firmly established.

Of course, the conclusion that advocates of the Law of Comparative Advantage draw from their analysis is that free trade, uninhibited by any sort of "artificial" barriers established by governments, is to the best interest of all concerned. Any interference with freedom of trade, they argue, will decrease not only the total amount of goods exchanged but also the total amount produced, since part of the energies of every country will be devoted to production of goods they could obtain with less effort from abroad.

The economists and statesmen of the underdeveloped countries by and large do not share this faith in the Law of Comparative Advantage and free trade. Quite to the contrary, they know that if they are to increase the production and income of their nations, and if they are to develop somewhat more balanced economies less subject to the violent changes originating in the already industrialized nations, they must offer protection to the newly developing industries within their borders. They realize, too, that the net result of a wise protectionist policy in their nations will not be to decrease world trade but to increase it. New industries will employ more people at higher incomes than were earned in traditional occupations.

At least part of this increased income will be spent to buy goods from abroad that the people of the underdeveloped countries could never previously purchase. Finally, they know that their countries do not have available the unlimited time the free traders insist that they must wait before their "natural advantage" for industries they do not now possess becomes obvious.

The underdeveloped nations of today have before them the great historical precedent of the developing nations of the nineteenth century. Over a century ago, the great German economist Friedrich List protested that the Law of Comparative Advantage was a British doctrine, designed to prevent the growth of other industrial nations that might destroy Great Britain's world monopoly of manufacturing.* Both Germany and the United States took List's words to heart and followed a protectionist policy during most of the latter half of the nineteenth century.† In retrospect it is difficult—in spite of the protests of many British, German, and American economists of that time and since—to declare that the United States and Germany were wrong in the policy they pursued.

THE "INFANT INDUSTRY" ARGUMENT

There are many reasons why the developing countries of the mid-twentieth century are justified in providing protection for their new industries. The simplest, and perhaps most widely accepted, argument was presented by the great Liberal econ-

* It is worth while noting that List got most of his ideas and arguments from two distinguished Americans, Alexander Hamilton and the economist Mathew Carey.

† Germany protected agriculture as well as industry, a move List deplored.

omist John Stuart Mill more than a century ago. It is the so-called "infant industry" argument. In today's underdeveloped countries it is particularly relevant.

There is no doubt that an entrepreneur seeking to establish a new industry, even a new industry whose products in time may be able to compete with imports, will in the beginning frequently find that his costs are much higher than those of similar plants in already industrialized countries. He will find that he will not have available those so-called "external econ-omies" that are taken for granted in the industrial nations. He may well have to provide his own power supply, build extensive transportation facilities, provide housing and hospital services for his workers and schools for their children—all things that are provided by society in general in a country that is already industrialized. He may have to develop his own sources of raw materials, and he will have to establish his own marketing facilities in the country, whereas his counterpart in a highly industrialized country can use those already in existence. He will in all likelihood find that necessary credit is difficult to obtain, and expensive.

In addition to this lack of "external economies," however, the new entrepreneur in a developing country will encounter still other handicaps to add to his costs during the first years of operation. He will not have available, in all probability, a skilled and disciplined labor force. Rather, he will have to hire a fair portion of his work force from migrants from the countryside who know little or nothing of machinery and have no experience with the relatively rigid discipline of the factory. It may take a whole generation before he has a really trained group of workers under his command. And unlike those who began industries in the United States or Britain, for instance, he will probably find from the beginning that he has to deal with trade unions and has to add the costs of social security and other labor legislation to his basic wage bill.

Furthermore, he will lack proper managerial talent. Very possibly, he himself will be a self-made manager or entrepreneur, with little practical experience in the industry in which he is establishing himself. Even if such be not the case, he will find only a small pool of trained middle and lower supervisory talent from which to draw. He will probably have to pay relatively higher salaries to obtain adequate managers—and may even have to bring in very expensive foreign personnel —than would be the case in an industrialized nation where such people were more readily and cheaply available. All these factors will add to his original investment. They will for some time be continuing costs he will have to bear. They will make his goods more costly than comparable products turned out in an already industrialized country that has available most of the factors the entrepreneur in an underdeveloped country will need to provide for himself. He can undertake to establish his new plant only if he is assured that he will be protected against foreign competition during a period long enough to allow him to absorb these costs.

THE ''BALANCED ECONOMY'' ARGUMENT

Even many advocates of universal free trade will accept the arguments we have just given. However, the case for protection in the developing countries goes a good deal further than this. There are many cases in which protection is justifiable even for industries that will never be able to compete with imports. Certainly most economists and politicians in the developing countries would support the protection of an industry that made a sizable contribution to the establishment

of a more balanced economy.* We have noted elsewhere †
that the underdeveloped countries, being producers of raw
materials and foodstuffs for export, frequently have found
themselves for one reason or another cut off from their sources
of imported manufactured goods. This has meant that textiles,
processed foodstuffs, and other things needed for the consumption of the general population have not been available.
Even when they have not been cut off from their sources of
supply, these nations have found that frequent and violent
price changes of their own export products have altered their
ability to purchase imports. As a result, the ability of their
people to obtain essential consumers' goods has been at the
mercy of international markets and price movements over
which an individual underdeveloped country has had little or
no control.

An underdeveloped nation is justified therefore in extending
protection to industries that will provide as many as possible
of the basic goods the consumers of the nation are going to
need regardless of whether there is a war in Europe, a depression in the United States, or whether the prices of the country's
major export are good or bad. Industries producing textiles
certainly rank high on the list of such commodities. So does
shoemaking. So do those industries making processed foodstuffs, such as meats, canned goods, flour.

The same argument can be extended to industries producing
building supplies. Cement production, sawmills and other
lumber industries, and some kinds of metallurgy—that producing steel rods for use in reinforced concrete construction, for
example—are certainly in this category. Not only do these

* Alexander Hamilton was one of the first to put forth this argument in his famous *Report on Manufactures*.
† See Chapter Two.

industries provide the material that is going to be needed for construction of houses and other necessary buildings; they also make possible at least on a limited scale government programs of public works in case of an economic slump, as well as programs of economic development.

Protection for these industries is justified not only because they produce goods that are going to be needed regardless of the state of the country's foreign economic relations but also because they will provide a more or less stable base of urban employment. If the whole of the country's economy orbits around the production and shipping of the principal export product and the import of goods paid for by this product, there will be little element of stability in employment or income. However, a solid base of manufacturing industry supplying the local market will provide at least a minimum element of stability.

Of course, the argument of a balanced economy can be exploited and misused, and this has occurred in a number of countries. Mexico has limited the entry of new and more efficient firms into the country's antiquated textile industry on the grounds that their entry will create unemployment, and as a result the Mexican textile industry has been in a state of crisis, and is sometimes unable to meet foreign competition even over a high tariff wall.

Chile has had a somewhat similar experience with the shoe-making industry. This trade was dominated until recently by craftsmen, making shoes largely by hand. The government showed more than the necessary amount of caution in allowing the importation of shoe machinery to modernize the industry —again on the grounds of fear of creating unemployment among artisan shoemakers.

These abuses, however, do not impair the validity of the

balanced-economy argument as a defense of protection for industry in the underdeveloped countries. Protective devices, like any other instrument of public policy, are most effective when used judiciously.

Another argument for protection of industries in developing countries that is even less accepted by the free traders than the balanced-economy case is that protection should be extended to industries that save an appreciable amount of foreign exchange. Here again, in the best of all possible worlds, this argument would have little validity, but in the kind of world in which the underdeveloped countries find themselves today, it has much merit.

Most developing nations have a more or less severe shortage of foreign exchange. The foreign currency available to them is by no means adequate to permit them to purchase all the goods they need to buy from the highly industrialized nations. In the face of such a shortage of foreign exchange, a developing nation may well be justified in protecting an industry the products of which may never be able to compete with foreign imports, if that industry will allow the country to divert sizable amounts of foreign exchange into the purchase of other much-needed products it could not otherwise obtain. Thus, for instance, when it was proposed to establish a steel industry in Chile during World War II, arguments were made that even if that industry were to need considerable protection for an indefinite period, it would be worth while because it would produce substitutes for $100,000,000 worth of imports a year. It would thus make it possible to spend an amount equivalent to about 10 per cent of the country's total yearly foreign exchange resources for things Chile otherwise would not be able to purchase. In such a case, although the cost of the good produced by such a protected industry might be somewhat greater in terms of local currency than similar products bought abroad, the production of such a good locally would make it possible for the underdeveloped country to enjoy the benefits of goods it could not otherwise have at all.

There is no doubt that this argument also is subject to abuse. Its validity in any given case must depend in part upon the amount of foreign currency that will be saved, as well as upon the degree to which the imposition of protective measures would increase the cost of the good in question. One Chilean writer has suggested that in the case of the steel plant, protection would have been justified if the price of steel was increased by no more than 25 per cent, but would not be warranted if the increase were more than that. One does not have to accept this somewhat arbitrary figure, but common sense dictates that a limit must be placed somewhere.

EFFECT OF PROTECTION ON INTER-NATIONAL TRADE

The crowning argument against protectionism by the devotees of the Law of Comparative Advantage is that it reduces the volume of international trade, and in so doing limits international specialization of labor and reduces the amount of goods available to the people of all countries. This argument certainly does not apply in the case of protection of basic consumers' goods industries in the underdeveloped countries.

The noted Argentine economist Raúl Prebisch, chief of the United Nations Economic Commission for Latin America, has pointed out on various occasions that in fact protectionism in the underdeveloped nations does not reduce the total volume of world trade. He argues that most of the trade of the underdeveloped nations is with one or another of the industrialized powers and that there is very little commerce among the underdeveloped nations themselves. He notes further that the volume of the trade between an underdeveloped country and an industrialized nation is determined by the industrialized country, not by the underdeveloped one. It depends, Dr. Prebisch says, on the willingness of the industrial nation to purchase the raw materials or the foodstuffs of the underdeveloped country.

Thus, if the industrial nation buys more copper or wool or coffee from its underdeveloped trading partner, the latter has more foreign exchange available to buy needed manufactured consumer wares, capital goods, or other commodities. If the industrial power reduces its purchases, the underdeveloped nation fatally must do likewise, since it will have less foreign exchange available to spend.

The raw-material- and foodstuff-producing nations generally cannot individually or jointly have significant influence on the amount of their products the industrialized nations will be willing to buy. The volume of raw material and foodstuff imports by the industrial countries depends on the state of economic activity in those countries. If they are prosperous, they will import more from the raw-material- and foodstuff-producing countries; if their economies are in the doldrums this will be reflected in a reduction of their purchases of raw materials and food abroad. Thus, for instance, if more cars are being made, more chrome, soy beans, natural rubber, and other products will be imported; if the auto industry is having a hard time selling its cars it will have a smaller demand for these imports from the underdeveloped countries.

There is little that the underdeveloped nations can do about this situation. The cutting of the prices of their export products —were this feasible—would not generally bring about an increase in the sales of these products if the business situation in the highly industrialized power were slumping; on the other hand, an increase in prices of raw materials or foodstuffs will not generally discourage their sale to the industrial countries if business is booming there.

Thus, the volume of international trade is determined basically by the highly industrialized powers, not by the underdeveloped nations. Furthermore, the potential demand of the underdeveloped countries for the goods of the highly industrialized ones at this stage in history is virtually insatiable. It is limited only by the availability to the underdeveloped nations of the currencies of the developed ones, with which to purchase the goods that are wanted. The availability of these currencies, in turn, is determined by the volume of purchases the industrialized nations make from their less-developed neighbors.

The effect of protection of a given industry in a developing country, therefore, will not be to reduce the amount that that country will buy from its industrial trading partner, and thus to reduce world trade. Rather, the effect will be to divert the underdeveloped nation's purchases from the product that was formerly imported, but is now being produced at home, to some other much desired commodity. The result of protectionism in underdeveloped nations will thus be to change the kinds of goods being traded, not to reduce the total volume of trade.

As the underdeveloped countries increasingly protect their textile, food-processing, and cement industries, for instance, it can be expected that the foreign exchange formerly spent on these products will be spent on the importation of capital equipment or of consumers' goods which could not be brought in at all before. The total value of goods imported will not change; merely the type of goods will be altered.

Indeed, over the long run protectionism in the underdeveloped countries can be expected to increase rather than to reduce the volume of world trade. As manufacturing industries are built up in the underdeveloped countries, increasingly large numbers of workers will be diverted from relatively unproductive agriculture to relatively productive manufacturing; as their output rises, their income will also rise. As their income rises, the new industrial workers' demand for consumers' goods, including those that are still imported, will increase. In general the increased rhythm of economic activity in the developing nation will be reflected in an increase in its demand for goods from abroad. Large segments of the population who were not in the market—domestic or foreign—will now receive money income and will purchase manufactured goods of various kinds. Many of these goods will still have to come from abroad. Only a few of the presently underdeveloped nations are ever likely to be in a position to be anywhere near self-sufficient.

These are all arguments that are familiar in the underdeveloped nations. In recent years they have been expressed with increasing insistence in various international forums by economists and politicians from the developing nations. They are sufficient answers to the universal pretensions of the Law of Comparative Advantage and the free traders.

TYPES OF PROTECTION

The question remains concerning what types of protectionism are best suited to the underdeveloped or developing countries. On this question, too, there has been a good deal of mystification on the part of some economists and politicians of the already industrialized nations, particularly in the United States. Spokesmen for the United States in international conferences—as well as many professors in their classrooms—have argued at great length to the effect that *if* there must be protection in the underdeveloped countries, it should be provided through the good old-fashioned mechanism of tariff duties. By no means should the underdeveloped countries—or anyone else for that matter—provide protection by quotas, exchange controls, or any other such unorthodox devices. One is tempted to think that the real burden of this argument is that since the United States in the heyday of its protectionism used tariffs, they are all right, but since exchange controls and quotas had not come into fashion when the United States was a high protectionist country, and hence were not used by the United States, they are somehow outside the pale. There is something ungentlemanly about their use—or so the argument runs. This argument has a good deal more appeal in the United States than in the developing countries, for reasons we shall explore.

Very simply, let us look for a moment at just what the various systems of protection are that might be used by the developing nations. First, and most orthodox, is the tariff, or tax upon imports. A government desirous of protecting a given industry will levy a tax on the importation of foreign goods competing with those of that industry, a tax sufficiently high to put the imported product at a decided disadvantage in the local market. This serves, of course, to give the local producers a sheltered market, and to keep out the bulk of foreign imports of this product.

An alternative to the protective tariff is a system of quotas or embargoes. There are many variations of this mechanism.

Imports may be limited to an amount sufficient to supply only that part of the local market that cannot be provided for by local industry. Or, on the plea of limiting imports to "essentials," or perhaps on the franker basis of seeking to protect a rival local industry, imports of certain products may be entirely prohibited. Or, perhaps, a licensing requirement for all imports may be established, and without any formal ruling, importers of certain goods competing with local industries may find it exceedingly difficult to get the necessary license. The bureaucratic mind is capable of divising almost infinite variations on the theme of quotas and embargoes.

An underdeveloped nation may also use exchange controls to limit competition from abroad for local industries. This procedure is perhaps most self-righteously condemned by the economists, civil servants, and politicians of the United States—largely, perhaps, because it has never been resorted to by this country. However, as many underdeveloped countries have found, exchange controls are frequently a highly effective method of extending protection.

Most of those countries using exchange controls for the purpose of protecting industry more or less stumbled upon them during the Great Depression of the 1930's. At that time all countries producing raw materials and foodstuffs found it exceedingly difficult to sell their products to the crisis-stricken industrial powers, and as a result were able to earn only very small amounts of foreign currency with which to pay for goods needed from abroad. They found themselves forced to ration this scarce currency. This was generally done by transferring all dealings in foreign exchange to the nation's Central Bank, and then establishing a sliding scale of exchange rates between the local currency and various foreign currencies.

How this worked out can be demonstrated by the case of Chile. During the 1930's Chile had three different exchange rates. Those importers who sought to bring in goods deemed "essential" were allowed to buy dollars at the cost of 19 pesos to the dollar. Those who wanted to bring in goods not deemed essential were forced to pay 31 pesos to get each dollar. Those who wanted to import goods the government did not particularly want brought in at all had to buy their foreign exchange in the euphemistically labeled "free market," where the rate varied but was considerably higher than 31 to the dollar.

Although this system was originally installed for the innocent purpose of rationing scarce foreign exchange, the government of the underdeveloped countries soon found that it was a very efficient vehicle for protection. All that was necessary to increase the cost of an imported good competing with locally manufactured produce was to change that import from the "essential" to the "unessential" category, thus considerably increasing the cost in terms of local currency of that import. Once aware of the potentialities of exchange control as a protective device, many underdeveloped countries began to use it deliberately for this purpose. However, in recent years, as the result in part at least of constant pressure from the United States, many countries have tended to reduce their reliance on exchange controls for protection.

It does not seem to the author that there is anything intrinsically right or wrong with any of these devices. Which one, if any, should be used would seem to depend upon the circumstances of time and place. In some of the underdeveloped countries with long and unguarded frontiers, where smuggling is easy, it might be easier to use exchange controls than to use tariffs as a means of protecting local industry. In other instances, exchange controls with their accompanying red tape, bureaucracy, and perhaps corruption, might serve as such a serious impediment to the importation of even those goods the governments was anxious to bring in that tariffs might be more advisable. In still other instances, outright prohibition of the entry of certain products from abroad might be the simplest measure to impose. Convenience and the general impact on the economy, rather than abstract theory, should be the guides as to which protective measure should be used.

Regardless of what device is decided upon for protection, virtually all underdeveloped nations feel that they must aid some of their local manufacturing industries. One who is concerned with the welfare and development of these nations cannot help agreeing with this position.

4

Planning and Economic Development

One of the characteristic features of economic growth in the contemporary less developed countries is planning. Perón had his five-year plans in Argentina; the Chilean Development Corporation soon after its establishment developed a twenty-five-year plan; Nehru's India is now at the beginning of its third five-year plan; even before achieving its independence, the West African state of Ghana had a three-year "emergency" plan, and soon after independence in 1957 began work on a longer-range program.

One of the most notable aspects of this penchant for planning by the economically developing nations is that ideology has little to do with it. Only a small minority of the governments of the underdeveloped nations profess belief in Socialism, but virtually all of them follow the practice of planning their economic development. It is obvious that their belief in planning arises from a deeply felt need, not from any particular doctrine.

There are several factors underlying this need: the developing countries are in a hurry and want rapid economic growth; they realize that without a concentrated effort toward economic development the gap between them and the already industrialized nations well may widen instead of narrowing; they appreciate the necessity to ration scarce resources of raw materials, foreign exchange, and other essentials for the development process.

PLANNING FOR RAPID DEVELOPMENT

The developing countries feel that they cannot wait for the "normal" processes of growth to take place. Looking at the economic history of Great Britain and the United States, among other industrialized nations, they see that in the former case the development of an industrial society took a century or more, and the process was preceded by two more centuries of preparation. In the case of the United States, economic development came somewhat more rapidly, lasting perhaps seventy-five years. However, most presently developing nations do not have the abundance of resources readily available that the United States possessed, and they realize that without central direction they could not hope to develop even as rapidly as the United States did.

Unwilling to wait for the workings of the untrammeled market to bring about industrial development, the economically less advanced nations, therefore, attempt to hasten the process by a greater or less degree of government-directed central planning. This is made more necessary by the definite possibility that without central planning the underdeveloped nations' economies might not develop at all. Gunnar Myrdal in his little book *Rich Lands and Poor* has suggested that the tendency of so-called "natural" economic forces is to widen the gap between the industrialized and the unindustrialized nations. He bases this idea on the belief that processes of social development, including those in the economic sphere, tend to be spiral-like and cumulative. That is to say, no nation's economy is likely to stand still, and if it once begins to move in other directions—toward development or toward regression —there is a tendency for such a movement to grow upon itself.

A factor that weighs heavily in favor of Dr. Myrdal's argument is the rapidly increasing population that characterizes most underdeveloped nations. Improved public health services in virtually all countries have quickly and dramatically reduced death rates. However, birth rates remain high and are dropping only slowly when at all. The effect of this situation is a rapid rise in population. Unless something drastic is done to increase the underdeveloped country's productive ability and diversify its economy, it is likely to be faced with the prospect of a decline in per capita income.

CUMULATIVE EFFECT OF GROWTH AND DECLINE

In an underdeveloped, largely agricultural nation its very poverty limits the market, and discourages would-be enterprisers from establishing new sources of production and income. This is intensified by the fact that in an underdeveloped country the taxation system is inevitably regressive (falling hardest on those with the lowest incomes), thus still further restricting the potential market. Any increase in population under these circumstances merely tends to intensify the poverty already existing, rather than acting as a stimulus to economic development. It leads to overcrowding on the land, with its consequent evils of erosion and destruction of the riches of the soil—the country's major source of wealth—and thus intensifying poverty, reducing the market still further, and hampering any improvement in the situation. Intense poverty makes possible the further exploitation of the poor through usurious interest rates, crushingly high rents, and other abuses—all of this tending to lead to concentration of ownership of land, the reduction of the mass of the rural population to a semifeudal condition, and putting them largely outside the market, that is, in a situation where they get little or no money income, but get their livelihood from agricultural activities that give them mere subsistence.*

The process of economic development also tends to grow upon itself. The introduction of new factories, or the opening up of other economic activities, tends to expand the market, thus making possible the building of still further industries to fill expanded needs. The growth of one kind of economic activity tends to provide the "external" economies—that is, the services and products—needed by others. Under these circumstances increasingly large numbers of people are drawn into occupations where they earn a money income, thus further expanding the market. Even an increase in population—which in a situation without economic development is a curse—acts as a stimulus to still further development to satisfy the needs of the increased numbers of people. As the pace of economic

* A recent study of Algeria, *Algeria: The Realities*, by Germaine Tillion indicates that what we have described is exactly what has occurred in that country during the last quarter of a century.

activity hastens, the burden of taxation can be spread over a wider group of people. The political position of the old aristocratic groups that have been able to avoid taxation, even though they had the highest incomes, tends to be weakened, and they can increasingly be forced to pay their share. Government income can rise, making possible further expenditures in providing the "social capital"—schools, hospitals, highways —a healthy society needs.

Facts indicate that the situation Dr. Myrdal discusses is true in the world today. The Report of the Special Studies Project of the Rockefeller Brothers Fund, published in the New York *Times* on June 16, 1958, gives strong evidence of this. It says:

"If recent trends in the world economy should continue, we would see the growth rates in total production of goods and services of:

"4 per cent in the United States.

"5 per cent in other free industrial countries, including Western Europe, Canada and Japan.

"3 per cent in Latin America and perhaps 2 per cent in other less developed areas.

"6 per cent in the Soviet Union, 3 per cent in the satellites and 2 per cent in Red China.

"If these growth rates are regrouped by broader categories, we get these results:

"4.5 per cent in free world industrial nations.

"4.5 per cent in the Communist bloc.

"2.5 per cent in less developed nations.

"The broad conclusion that emerges from these projections is that existing economic disparities among nations would widen. . . ."

The same report gives an indication of why the gap between

developed and underdeveloped nations will tend to widen. It notes that the "free world industrial nations" in 1955 devoted 80 per cent of their output to the supply of civilian wants and military purposes, while the "less industrialized areas" devoted 87 per cent to those purposes. The industrialized powers had a rate of investment—that is, addition to their capital equipment—of 20 per cent of their total production, and the less industrialized nations had an investment rate of only 13 per cent. All this means that the gap between the highly industrialized nations and the underdeveloped countries is widening.

In order to prevent this breach from continuing to widen, it is not enough to rely on "natural" forces of development. In most underdeveloped countries the search for raw materials and foodstuffs by firms from the industrialized countries provided the first impetus for development. Modern mining and agricultural enterprises were established, and usually improved transportation facilities were developed to serve them. The whole temper of economic activity was heightened.

However, in many if not most of the underdeveloped countries these activities have tended to remain on the periphery of the economy. The great masses of the people remain untouched—particularly if the additional income coming into the national economy of the underdeveloped nation has been spent mainly on providing still more luxury goods for those who were already purchasing these before the expansion of production of minerals or agricultural raw materials began.

During recent decades the two world wars and the Great Depression acted as spurs toward economic development. However, the underdeveloped countries cannot be expected to wait for foreign firms to seek investment opportunities, or for wars and depressions, for their future economic expansion. The problem facing most underdeveloped countries is that they desire to develop their economies rapidly. They cannot afford to wait for "natural" phenomena to bring such development about. For this, positive action is required.

PLANNING FOR ECONOMIC USE OF RESOURCES

A planned program for economic development provides such positive action. It not only consciously pumps investment capital, know-how, and other essentials to economic development into a lagging economy; it also makes it possible to use the limited resources available to a newly developing nation most effectively and economically. It makes it possible to divert foreign exchange income arising from exports of raw materials and foodstuffs into capital importation and development of technical skills instead of luxury consumption.

In a few countries central government planning is stimulated by the fact that the state receives a large part of the national income. In some petroleum-producing nations oil revenues make up a major part of the total income of the nations, and the governments receive a sizable part of such revenues. Iraq, Iran, and Venezuela are in this category.

None of the countries outside the Iron and Bamboo curtains have attempted the Soviet Union's kind of extremely intricate and detailed planning. The U.S.S.R. has attempted to plan the output of virtually every factory, farm, and other enterprise within its borders. Prices and wages have been set by the planning authorities, and each enterprise has been instructed where to acquire its raw materials and where to sell its output. However, even the Communist nations have come to realize that trying to plan the output of every enterprise, without allowing prices to be determined by market forces of supply and demand, has more handicaps than advantages. They are in the process of modifying that system.

Planning in non-Communist countries of Asia, Africa, and Latin America is of a different nature. The government generally has not fixed prices or wages. It has left the producers to get their raw materials wherever most advantageous to them, and to sell their goods wherever most profitable. In any case, the underdeveloped nations would find it difficult to engage in exceedingly minute planning even if they wished to do so. Statistics tend to be notoriously scarce and unreliable, and until a nation's development efforts are well under way a government would not have sufficient dependable information upon which to do more than very general programing.

METHODS OF PLANNING

The basic objective of planning in most of these countries is to coordinate otherwise independent and separate economic decisions for rapid growth. The planners try to assure that a sufficiently large part of the national income is channeled into the accumulation of capital equipment to build a more varied economy, able to provide a higher material standard of living for the citizenry.

The planning agencies in these countries begin by estimating and analyzing the national income, including its economic development aspects. They then try to lay out a series of development projects, in agriculture, industry, the public services, and other fields, matching those projects with likely resources from private and public sources within the country as well as from abroad. The efforts of private agriculturalists, industrialists, mercantile interests, and public-utility firms are thus coordinated with those of public-works ministries and government-development institutions.

The periodical three- or five- or seven-year plans set certain goals to be achieved by their completion. These goals are set in terms of growth of the national income, as well as in terms of individual projects. Not infrequently, it is found necessary to modify these goals before the completion of the plan, as in the case of India's Second Five-Year Plan, which had to be revised downward early in 1958.

Usually the plans take into account not only the need for agricultural, industrial, mining, commercial, and public-works projects but also provide for building up the nation's "social capital" as well. Thus, expansion of regular school systems (including school construction, training of personnel, and general educational policy), programs for training needed specialists, housing development, hospital building projects, and similar programs are included in the over-all plans.

On the basis of the general plan, the governments involved determine other aspects of their over-all economic policy. Taxation, for instance, is modified, insofar as possible, so as to raise needed revenue for the government's contributions to the plan, as well as to encourage private economic activities in conformity with the planning objectives and discouraging those that conflict with them. Foreign exchange control, if it is needed, is adapted to make it easier to import those goods necessary for the plan, and more difficult to bring in those that might hinder its development. Tariffs and other protective devices are adopted to support those industries to be encouraged during the period of the plan. General foreign economic relations are designed to strengthen the government's planning objectives.

One of the principal purposes of central planning for economic development has been the rationing of scarce resources. The "free" and "natural" processes of the economy are interfered with by the planning authorities so that the foreign exchange, internal capital resources, raw materials, skilled labor, and other factors needed for the process of economic growth are made available for that purpose. Otherwise, these resources might merely stimulate conspicuous consumption by the upper classes or be used in other activities that would make little or no contribution to economic development.

Four examples of national planning efforts will serve to illustrate the purpose, nature, and problems of these phenomena. We shall note the plans of the Chilean Development Corporation, the new nation of Ghana, the Republic of India, and the semiautonomous Commonwealth of Puerto Rico.

Chilean planning

Chile was one of the first of the underdeveloped nations to draw up and put into execution a development plan. It varied in many ways from those that have subsequently become general, but it had some aspects in common with them, too.

The Chilean Development Corporation was established in 1939. During its first months it drew up a detailed plan of operations for twenty-five years in advance. This program was divided into three different sections, dealing respectively with power resources, agriculture, and manufacturing industry. The first part proposed to develop the very large resources for hydroelectric power present in the mountainous republic. It proposed the establishment of a government power-and-light firm, the Empresa Nacional de Electricidad S.A., through which the corporation would operate. A series of projects spread the length of the country were to be coordinated with other phases of economic development, with first attention being paid to the region around the city of

Concepción, near which it was proposed to establish an iron and steel plant. The ultimate objective has been to establish a nation-wide electric grid.

In the field of agricultural development, the ambitions of the corporation were more limited. Its efforts were principally to be directed toward facilitating the entry of implements and machinery to modernize the country's generally antiquated farming methods. Its success in this field has been relatively limited.

In manufacturing, the corporation made its first impressive showing. The firm began an extensive program of lending to, investing in, and otherwise helping the growth of a wide range of firms in the metal industry, pharmaceuticals and chemicals, and other fields.

In all phases of its program, the corporation has acted as a clearing agency for obtaining foreign loans and investments. Thus, for instance, the corporation raised loans from the Export-Import Bank of the United States for the new steel plant that it constructed. It arranged with the General Tire Company of the United States to join with it in establishing the Industria Nacional de Neumáticos, to make automobile tires and other rubber products. It aided several Chilean firms to make contact with United States enterprises that were willing to invest and help them expand their activities.

The net effect of the development planning of the corporation has been to be a kind of catalyst for Chilean economic growth. Not only did the corporation directly encourage private enterprise to enter or expand their operations in a number of industries; the firms set up or aided by the corporation also indirectly provided opportunities for many other private investors. For instance, it is estimated that the steel fabricating industry more than doubled in output during the half-dozen years following the opening of the corporation's steel plant at Talcahuano.

The planning operation of the Chilean Development Corporation differs from most other similar efforts in that the corporation has not attempted to plan the economy as a whole. It has chosen a series of objectives for its own operations, without exercising any general control over the economy, as the planning authority in most underdeveloped nations do. Although the Chilean government has sometimes coordinated other programs with that of the corporation, the latter has not had over-all supervision of the economic development program.

Planning in Ghana

The West African nation of Ghana, while still a semi-autonomous crown colony of Great Britain, adopted a three-year emergency development plan. The purpose of this program was to lay the basis for a series of more extensive and complex plans in the future. It included attempts to rationalize the production of the country's principal export crop, cocoa, as well as to stimulate the growth of other agricultural exports. It also included a comprehensive program of building communications, transport and port facilities, and a "crash program" for extending the country's educational system. It also laid emphasis on the operations of the Industrial Development Corporation, which built a number of small manufacturing enterprises throughout the country and sought to encourage foreign investors to establish others. Great emphasis was laid on the development of technical skills and know-how on the part of the citizens of Ghana.

One of the most ambitious parts of this emergency program

of Ghana was preliminary work on a vast project to dam the Volta, the principal river in the country. This project was studied by officials of Canadian and American aluminum companies as well as United States and British government agencies and the World Bank. It was to be designed to produce vast quantities of electric power, which would be the basis for an industry to process the country's sizable resources of bauxite, in addition to supplying the light and power needs of a large part of the country. It was also to be designed to promote irrigation and to fight against the ever-menacing encroachment of the Sahara Desert from the north.

This program still had a year or more to run when Ghana received its independence early in 1957. A year later the government put the finishing touches on a more comprehensive five-year development plan, which had as one of its cornerstones the actual launching of the Volta River Project. At the end of 1961 final arrangements were finally reached with the United States and British governments, the International Bank for Reconstruction and Development, and British and Canadian aluminum companies for financing this Project.

Indian plans

One of the most ambitious programs of economic planning in the non-Communist world has been that of the Republic of India. The First Indian Five-Year Plan was begun in 1951 and was completed five years later. Its principal emphasis was on an expansion of the country's agriculture. The leaders of the Indian government felt that their most pressing immediate problem was to make some progress in the race between the nation's rapidly rising population and its food production. Vast TVA-like irrigation projects were undertaken;

large areas were reclaimed from destructive grasses that had wiped out agriculture in considerable areas; and new lands were put into cultivation in what had been forest regions.

This aspect of the First Five-Year Plan seemed to have been successful at the time the plan came to an end. Agricultural output had increased considerably more than the population— though to what degree this was due to the plan and to what degree it was due to a series of exceedingly good years, climatically speaking, was a matter of dispute both inside India and abroad.

The First Five-Year Plan laid some emphasis, too, on improvement of transportation facilities and on the development of manufacturing industry. Large loans were obtained from the International Bank for Reconstruction and Development for the purpose of reequipping the railroads and improving their track. Both the government and private firms undertook to expand the nation's iron and steel production. Agreements were signed with British and United States oil companies to establish large refineries in the country.

A unique aspect of the Indian Five-Year Plan was the emphasis put on community development projects. With the help of United States foundations and the Point Four Program, a start was made toward the goal of establishing such a project in every Indian village. The principle upon which these operate is that of encouraging the villagers to help themselves. Teams are sent into individual villages to survey the area and to gain the confidence of the inhabitants. They are asked what the particular needs of their village are, and then the villagers are encouraged to set to work to provide them for themselves, the government standing ready to extend aid in the form of materials, technical skill, and supervision. The community development program ran into many difficulties in terms of problems of recruiting adequate personnel, tendencies to get bogged down in government red tape, and sabotage of the program by some vested interests in the villages themselves. However, in spite of these handicaps, projects had been established in several thousand villages by the end of the First Five-Year Plan.

The Second Five-Year Plan of India was drawn up on a basis different from that of the first. Emphasis in this plan was laid on industry, particularly heavy industry. Programs were drawn up for the establishment of several large iron and steel plants and major expansion of existing ones. Aid in this aspect of the program was to be provided by several foreign countries, including Great Britain, West Germany, and the Soviet Union. Other heavy industries received equally large attention.

The reasoning of the Indian leaders was that all future industrialization of the nation would depend upon the republic's being able to supply most of its heavy industry needs, and the Second Five-Year Plan therefore was in the nature of a foundation stone for all plans to come. The possibility of India's importing its growing needs for iron, steel, and other products of heavy industry is very limited, since these needs will soon be too large for even the biggest exporters of these products to satisfy them. Furthermore, there are inherent dangers in having to depend too heavily on such imports, particularly as the country's needs grow.

An interesting controversy arose during the preparation of the Second Five-Year Plan. This centered upon the role that "cottage" industry—that is, handicraft industries in village homes—should play in the plan. Indian villagers have always produced a large part of the textiles and other consumers' products they have used. Since it is likely to be some time before most of the villagers have sufficient money income to purchase such goods in the market, it was felt by many that the Second Five-Year Plan should lay considerable emphasis on helping the villagers to produce more handicraft goods more efficiently. It was argued that this would result in an immediate increase in the real income and standard of living of the villagers. This line of reasoning was strengthened by memories of Gandhi's strong endorsement of cottage industries during the campaign for Indian independence.

Those who opposed the allocation of any appreciable part of the resources available under the plan to the stimulation of cottage industries argued that in the long run the building up of heavy industry was more important and that inevitably any resources diverted to cottage industries would be taken away from large-scale industry. They also feared that the development of factory industries producing consumers' goods would be slowed down, in an effort to prevent their competition with the village output of these products.

The first draft of the Second Five-Year Plan provided for very extensive help for the cottage industries of the villages. However, as the result of criticism both by Indian experts and foreign economic advisers, it was finally decided to allot considerably less importance to this aspect of development.

The final draft of the Second Five-Year Plan called for India to depend very heavily on foreign aid for the fulfillment of the plan. Indian officials were rather vague as to just where this aid would come from, but expressed confidence that it could be secured. However, by early 1958 it became obvious that these officials had been overly optimistic, and the country's reserves of foreign exchange were beginning to get dangerously low. As a result, it was found necessary to cut back rather substantially on the goals of the plan, to make it conform more closely to the actual resources available.

In 1961 the Third Indian Plan went into effect. It continued to lay great stress on industrialization. As it went into effect, the Third Plan seemed likely to mobilize a good deal more foreign help than had been available in the previous five years.

It is interesting to note that the efforts of both government-owned and private firms are coordinated in the Indian Five-Year plans. A considerable degree of emphasis is given to the development of government-owned enterprises, particularly in heavy industry. However, although these firms are the property of the state, there is no attempt to disrupt the normal operation of the market, and the government firms act just like private companies insofar as their purchases of raw materials and labor and the sale of their own products are concerned.

Planning in Puerto Rico

Planning in the island of Puerto Rico in the West Indies has been unique in several respects. First of all, it has been carried out by the government of an area that did not possess full independence and therefore did not have certain measures, such as tariff protection, available for its use. In the second place, Puerto Rico's planned development is one of the most thorough and integrated efforts of this kind in the non-Communist world. Finally, the development process has been a continuing program, without being divided into special "plans" of a given number of years.

Puerto Rico for half a century had been principally a producer of sugar for export to the continental United States. In 1940 there came to office a government in the island that wished to develop a more diversified economy, and although its efforts were at first hampered by the Second World War, they were pushed with great energy as soon as that conflict was over.

The effort of the Puerto Rican government toward development has been a well rounded one. It has sought expansion of manufacturing, diversification of agriculture, development of power resources, growth of the education system, improvement of public health services, provision of better housing, development of social security.

The over-all supervision of the development program is in the hands of the Planning Board. Its approval is necessary for the establishment of any capital improvement. There is a range of government organizations working with the Planning Board, which has changed somewhat from time to time. However, in 1962 the principal economic development instruments of the Puerto Rican government were the Economic Development Administration, the Development Corporation, the Government Development Bank, the Water Resources Authority, and the Land Authority.

The Economic Development Administration has the job of enticing new firms to come to the island—principally from the mainland United States. It helps prospective firms to obtain credit, land, and other needs for establishing their businesses in Puerto Rico, and arranges for tax exemption provided in the law for firms that qualify for it. It also helps firms deal with initial problems they encounter when coming to Puerto Rico, and keeps in touch with these firms at later stages. It maintains offices in the continental United States to carry on the missionary activity of convincing firms there to come to the island.

The Industrial Development Corporation has the key function of constructing buildings for new enterprises, particularly in areas away from San Juan, the capital. It has followed the policy of building standard types of buildings for prospective investors, though in specific cases it modifies these plants to suit the specific needs of new firms. In the San Juan area most factory buildings are constructed by private contractors.

The purpose of the Government Development Bank is to arrange loans to small firms, particularly those created by Puerto Ricans, although it does lend also to enterprises coming from the continent. It usually guarantees loans made by other credit institutions rather than actually lending the funds itself. It also has the additional responsibility of being the fiscal agent of the Puerto Rican government. As part of the United States, Puerto Rico does not have its own central bank, but the Development Bank is the nearest thing to such an institution.

The Water Resources Authority was created in the early 1940's for the purpose of creating an island-wide electricity network. It purchased the properities of two foreign-owned electric firms as the foundation for its program. Subsequently, it has built a number of hydroelectric projects, and the power system of the island has proved equal to the demands of a rapidly expanding economy.

The Land Authority, also established in the early 1940's, has had a varied program. The government carried out an extensive land-reform program, and the land expropriated under this program was turned over to the Authority. In the late 1940's the program of the defunct Agricultural Development Corporation, which had been set up to encourage a diversification of agriculture, was entrusted to the Authority.

Some of the job of coordinating the work of all these institutions, in addition to the building programs of the Health and Education Department, is done by the Planning Board. Before a building permit for a new manufacturing plant can be issued, the board must give its approval, and generally it makes sure that there is adequate power and transportation, and sufficient housing and school facilities to meet the needs of the plant and its workers. The board has further control over the general development program by its power to approve or disapprove all government capital investment projects.

This is probably the best organized and best directed program that any developing nation has had in recent years. Of course, it has enjoyed the advantages that Puerto Rico is a relatively small area and that its being part of the United States has made particularly feasible the attraction of investments to the island from the mainland.

SUMMARY

Central planning by the government has thus become an integral part of economic growth in the developing countries. It has been used by governments of widely differing ideology, and has been resorted to as a matter of necessity by widely differing governments, many of which have had in common only the fact that they were seeking rapid economic development. It has been a means of giving strong impetus to development, and of providing a considerable degree of coordination of public and of much private development activity. Planning has been a means, also, of channeling resources into those aspects of economic growth considered most pressing. A wide variety of methods has been used for drawing up and carrying out planning programs, although the system of successive "plans" for a given number of years has been the most popular procedure. Whatever method has been used, there is little doubt that central planning has become a key aspect of economic development.

5

Agrarian Problems and Economic Development

In many countries economic development is regarded as being virtually synonymous with industrialization. However, agriculture must be an integral part of any successful economic development program. Without parallel and simultaneous change and expansion of agriculture, industrial growth will be one-sided, excessively expensive, and will not achieve the aims its protagonists set for it.

From the viewpoint of economic development, there are two basic problems that must be dealt with in agriculture in most of the economically less advanced countries: agrarian reform, or the redistribution of land ownership; and the growth of agricultural productivity. In most cases, these two factors are closely intertwined and depend very much upon each other, as both depend on the process of industrialization.

The traditional patterns of landholding in most of the underdeveloped countries are a great drawback to economic development. In Latin America, for instance, most arable land is held by large landholders. In most cases the workers on the land are outside the money economy. They work their landlord's acres in return for the use of a small parcel of land upon which they grow by primitive methods the food their families consume. In some countries the tenants owe personal service to the landowner in addition to the obligation to work his land when and how he tells them to do.

AGRARIAN REFORM AND ECONOMIC DEVELOPMENT

Large landholding, or latifundia as it is often called, is also a curse of most of the other economically less developed nations. In India, for example, the British changed people who had been recognized in previous times only as tax farmers—collectors of taxes for the government in return for a share of the tax—into owners of the land from which they had previously collected taxes. Thus most of the cultivable land of the subcontinent came into the hands of relatively large landowners many of whom did not live on the land they held.

In many countries the problem of latifundia is complicated by population pressure, which gives rise to other serious problems. Where rural population is very large in comparison with the amount of land, each tenant has such a small piece to work that only in the best years can he grow enough to pay his rent and feed his family. Frequently he has to borrow from moneylenders to tide him over until the next harvest comes in. Usually both rent and interest under these conditions are very high. It is not unusual for small independent farmers to lose their land and be converted into tenants as the result of their inability to pay back loans and their exorbitant interest. Often, too, the tenant is called upon to pay the taxes on the land as well as the other charges. As a result, he goes deeper and deeper into debt and is less and less able to supply his family adequately. This is a perfect case of what Gunnar Myrdal refers to as the circular and cumulative impact of a social and economic process.

Traditional landholding systems thus often present two apparently contradictory tendencies: the division of the land into very small cultivating units, and the ownership of the land by a comparatively small group of people. In almost all underdeveloped countries there is at least one of these phenomena present.

These traditional forms of landownership are an important drawback to the economic development process. In the first place they seriously limit the market for the products of new industries. Tenants or independent farmers deeply in debt have very little money income. They live at a subsistence level, have very little of what they produce available to sell, and hence do not receive money payments. Thus, for instance, it has been estimated that of the seventy million people of Brazil, perhaps only thirty million are actually in the market to buy any appreciable amount of manufactured goods. In many of the economically less advanced countries, the proportion of the total population that remains outside the market is even greater than in the case of Brazil.

Thus, the lack of a market among the rural population makes it difficult for manufacturing industry to grow. It makes impossible the economies that come with large-scale production in almost all kinds of manufacturing. It makes certain kinds of industries absolutely impossible. Furthermore, traditional landholding patterns also hamper the development of agriculture itself. On the one hand, the large landholder who gets a good income from selling the part of the farm's products that are grown for and sold by him has little incentive to increase production or to introduce new methods into agriculture. One of the attributes of the large landholding system is usually conspicuous consumption. One of the reasons the landholder is a landholder is so that he will have an income he can spend lavishly. And, since his income is adequate, he sees no reason to restrict it by investing in capital equipment to expand production that he may have a still larger income in the future.

The large landholder generally has little interest, either, in investing in manufacturing industry. Indeed, it is frequently not socially acceptable for him to do so. In many cases, even if he had the desire to turn some of his capital into industrial investment he might well find himself unable to do so. In fact, many of the large landholders in the underdeveloped countries find that much of their income really consists of the unpaid labor they can exact from their tenants and workers. Even if they wanted to, they could not convert this into capital in anything other than agriculture.

If the landlords have little incentive to invest even in agriculture itself, or to expand production, the tenants have even less such incentive. Since virtually everything they produce goes to the landlord, their creditors, or the tax collector, most of the gains from any innovations or increased labor on their part will go to these groups, not to the tenants. Furthermore, not being owners of the land, the tenants find little reason why they should make capital improvements on what doesn't belong to them—even if they were to have the means to do so.

The upshot of this situation is that in many of the developing nations agriculture has lagged far behind other parts of the economy. The farms are unable to produce the food the growing populations of the cities require, thus making it necessary to use precious foreign currency that might be used in further economic development on the importation of foodstuffs. They are also unable to grow the raw materials that one might expect they could provide for the new manufacturing industries—thus cutting down on whatever savings in foreign exchange new factories may bring about.

In one other way, too, the continuance of the large landholding system is a drawback to economic development. It supports the political position of the landlord class, and gives them power out of all proportion to their numbers. With the absolute control that they are able to maintain over their tenants and workers, the landlords can march these people to the polls to vote for the candidates the landlords select. Frequently, the landlord class will use this power in legislatures and governments to prevent or at least hamper further industrialization. This was notoriously true of Argentina in the 1930's, when a landlord-controlled government did all it could to put industry at a disadvantage in that country.

EXTENT AND NATURE OF
AGRARIAN REFORM

Traditional forms of rural landlordship, therefore, are a serious handicap to a nation in the process of developing its economy. The redistribution of land, in one way or another, is a fundamental necessity for rapid growth not only of agriculture but also of manufacturing industry and other parts of the economy as well. It is by no means coincidental, therefore, that the period since World War II, which has seen such a flurry of economic development throughout the world, has also been characterized by a widespread movement for land reform. In Latin America, Bolivia, Guatemala, Venezuela, Colombia, Cuba, and Puerto Rico have undertaken such programs—while Mexico had virtually completed a revolutionary process of agrarian reform before the outbreak of World War II. In Africa the new revolutionary government of Egypt that took power in the early 1950's had land reform as one of its fundamental objectives. India, Pakistan, Burma, Korea, and Japan in Asia have undertaken more or less fundamental agrarian reforms. Indonesia, South Vietnam, and the Philippine Republic have attempted to move people off the latifundia onto unoccupied public lands.

Different circumstances have brought about different kinds of agrarian reform, and will do so in the future. In Mexico and Bolivia, where the land had been cultivated under semifeudal conditions of sharecropping and forced labor, the land was virtually confiscated by revolutionary governments and was placed in the hands of the workers who resided on it. In the case of Korea, areas belonging to large landowners were expropriated in return for bonds. These bonds, in turn, could be exchanged for stock in new industries being started in the urban areas.

In Burma, where the problem had been largely one of peasants falling under the control of moneylenders who were increasingly getting control of the land, the problem was partially resolved by the moneylenders, most of whom were Indians, fleeing the country during the Second World War. They were compensated for the lands they held; the land was then nationalized and granted to the peasants. At the same time credit facilities were provided for the peasantry, so that it would not again fall into the hands of usurers, and the government undertook to sell the country's principal crop and major export, rice, through a monopoly organization, the benefits of which were passed on to the farmers.

In many countries agrarian reform programs short of those of Mexico, Bolivia, or Korea are in order. For instance, the South American republic of Chile is faced with a situation in which approximately half of the arable land of her great Central Valley, which is the chief agricultural section of the country, is not cultivated by the large landholders who own most of it. It has been suggested that the appropriate measure to force the landowners to use their holdings is a tax on unused land, giving the present owners a time limit to put the land into use. Then the tax could be increased to 100 per cent if the land remained out of cultivation. Land acquired by the state in this way could then be turned over to farmers, including both Chileans and immigrants, willing to put it to work.

AGRICULTURAL DEVELOPMENT

Although the redistribution of the land is in many of the underdeveloped countries a fundamental requirement for rapid economic growth, it is nowhere sufficient. It is useful only if it is a prelude to agricultural development. There is a tendency in the developing countries to overlook the importance of this aspect of the problem. Indeed, in many countries the problem of development is discussed in terms of "economic development" (by which is meant industrialization) or "agriculture," as if the two were mutually exclusive. There is often little realization that manufacturing industries, communication;

transportation, and agriculture must march hand in hand in order to have a balanced and healthy development program.

There are at least four fundamental reasons why agricultural development is necessary as a part of a more general program of economic growth: because it is needed to provide the raw materials and foodstuffs for urban industries and their workers; because it can bear a share—through the export of agricultural products—of the cost of importing necessary capital equipment from abroad; because it frees labor for other parts of the economy that are growing; because it will provide a market for the products of industry.

As industry grows, the cities grow. Furthermore, as productivity of industry goes up, incomes go up as well. Hence, there is an increasing demand in the urban centers for foodstuffs. This is particularly true during the first phases of industrialization, while the workers are still getting paid relatively low wages. It is generally true that workers with low wages spend a disproportionate share of their income on food. For a while, therefore, as their incomes go up, a very large part of this increase will go for the purchase of more and better food.

At the same time, new manufacturing industries need raw materials. Many of these raw materials will be of agricultural origin. The textile industry, packing and canning, vegetable-oil processing, plastics, shoe and leather making are but a few of the branches of manufacturing that will use materials produced by the farmers.

If the food and raw-material needs of a newly industrializing country can be met from within that country, this will make it unnecessary to use foreign currencies, which the country earns with its exports, to purchase them from abroad. Foreign exchange can be used, instead, to buy more capital equipment and to buy those consumers' goods which the country needs but does not yet make for itself.

Agriculture can make an additional contribution to the process of urban development if it can swell the volume of the country's exports. If the country's agriculture can produce coffee, wheat, meat, cocoa, palm oil, hemp, or some other agricultural commodity for sale abroad, or can increase the amounts of these or other things it already produces for export, it can contribute to the country's foreign exchange resources.

This is one of the facts that is perhaps least understood in the underdeveloped countries. Since one of the reasons for industrialization is to get away from excessive dependence on a narrow range of export products, many people tend to think that the answer is to reduce the amount of export—or at least not to increase it. However, this attitude is shortsighted and absurd. The objective of economic development should be to stimulate the growth of other parts of the economy, not to limit or destroy those parts that are already in existence. Thus, where possible, a program of industrialization should be accompanied by a program of stimulating existing exports and trying to develop others. In the long run, success in this endeavor will mean that a larger proportion of the capital goods that must be obtained with foreign currencies can be purchased outright in return for commodities the country produces. Thus, the developing nation will have to depend that much less on foreign investments or foreign aid.

The development and modernization of agriculture can make an important contribution in yet another way. In some countries there is, in the beginning of the industrialization process at least, a shortage of workers for new manufacturing plants. The improvement of agricultural methods, particularly the use of new and better implements and even of machinery, will free many workers from rural labors, and make them available for work in the city. Both the worker and the economy are likely to gain from this process. The economy gains because it gets the transfer of a laborer from a field in which he is less productive to one in which he is more productive. The worker gains because he receives at least a part of the increase in his own productivity.

Finally, the growth of agriculture is important to economic development because it provides a market for the products of industry. Old-type subsistence agriculture that characterizes large parts of most of the underdeveloped countries does not provide any market at all for the products of industries. Farmers without money incomes cannot buy industrial products. However, if the agriculturalist produces more, if he has increasing amounts of products to sell to the city man, he can buy in return rising quantities of industrial products.

In this connection the processes of agrarian reform and of agricultural development are closely linked. If there has been no redistribution of land, and the income from increased agricultural ouput goes principally to the large landholding class, that class will have a tendency to spend it on luxury goods that are not made at home, or upon travel and expenditures abroad. On the other hand, if there has been a redistribution of the land, and the increased income arising from greater agricultural productivity goes into the hands of small farmers, they are most likely, at least for some time, to spend this increased income on simpler things, such as better clothes, improved housing, and other items that are first produced by a country in the early stages of economic development.

Increasing the productivity of agriculture in the underdeveloped nations is a complicated task. Indeed, in some countries it seems like an almost impossible one. There are so many things to be done that those attempting to attack the problem hardly know where to begin. However, it is possible to summarize the principal aspects of an agricultural development program.

AGRICULTURAL EXTENSION AND CREDIT

Fundamental to any such program is the establishment of some sort of extension service, that is, an organization that can teach farmers new methods on a more or less day-to-day business. Generally such a service has agents who live in farm areas and are kept currently informed concerning new methods of cultivation, new fertilizers, and other improvements in agriculture. They are in a position to visit individual farmers, to hold exhibitions, to give lectures, and to distribute literature to those farmers who can read it. Such a service is usually closely coordinated with a network of experiment stations, where new methods can be tried out and which farmers can visit and see for themselves how to improve their way of growing and taking care of their crops.

In many of the underdeveloped countries the United States Department of Agriculture's Extension Service has been used as a model for the establishment of similar institutions. One of the most important aspects of the United States' technical assistance program in the underdeveloped countries has been that of helping these nations to establish such services. India is one of the Asian countries that has been most interested in this program. In Latin America considerable progress has been made in setting up an extension service in Bolivia, among other countries. There, United States experts have helped to train local agents for the new service, to organize youth groups among the peasants—the local equivalent of 4-H Clubs—and have also helped to set up several experimental farms as part of the system.

Another essential to an agricultural development program is a system of cheap credit for the farmers. In almost all countries there are large numbers of farmers who find that they must borrow money in order to finance their crops, paying off these short-term debts when the harvest comes in. Farmers everywhere find a need, also, for longer-term credit, to help them purchase implements and machinery, to help them construct new buildings, and to aid in financing other capital improvements that involve the expenditure of a relatively large amount of money they cannot pay off by the proceeds of one harvest.

Hitherto, in most of the underdeveloped countries the farmers, when they have been able to get such loans at all, have had to turn to usurious moneylenders, who would lend to them only at very high rates of interest. The regular banking systems of these countries generally will not make such loans to small agriculturalists, on the grounds that they are too great a credit risk. Only the large landholders, therefore, are able to make use of the normal banking system.

Hence, an integral part of an agricultural development program must be the establishment by the government, or through cooperatives, of a system of cheap agricultural credit. In most cases this is done through one or more government banks, established specially for this purpose. However, in the case of Ceylon, the island nation south of India, the credit needs of the small farmers have been largely met by a network of cooperatives that have received some help from the government.

In some countries the government agricultural banks have also undertaken to sell the farmers' products. Whether or not this is done, it is necessary in most underdeveloped nations to establish some new kind of system for the farmer to bring his produce to market, and to assure him a more or less decent price for his output. Without such a system, the small farmer is at the mercy of large firms that buy up the crop immediately after harvesting, when the market is saturated and the products can be bought at very low prices. The large trader then sells these goods throughout the year, and reaps most of the profit from their production.

Many ways have been found to get around this problem. In Mexico, the so-called Ejido banks, which make loans to many of the small agriculturalists who have received land under the government's agrarian reform program, have frequently agreed to buy the farmer's products at fixed prices. In Burma the government has a special marketing agency that always stands ready to buy the agriculturalists' rice crop at a price agreed upon early in the growing season, though the farmers are free to sell their products to private traders if they can receive a better price from them.

MECHANIZATION AND MARKETING

A certain degree of mechanization is also necessary for a successful agricultural development program. The tools and implements used in most of the underdeveloped nations are exceedingly primitive and have not changed in hundreds of years. In most of these countries it is probably not feasible to jump from these antique methods of production to modern agricultural machines, since the peasants would not be in a position either to know how to use them or to be able to finance their purchase. However, a considerable increase in output can undoubtedly be achieved by improving old methods of production—introducing plows with metal tips, for instance, in place of wooden ones; introducing slightly improved instruments for harrowing and for harvesting the crop. Common sense is undoubtedly called for in this part of the agricultural development program, so as not to jump too far ahead of the farmer's ability to assimilate new methods.

One of the principal difficulties many farmers face in the underdeveloped nations is the problem of getting their crops to market. Road networks are inadequate, and do not reach many of the parts of the country where there are farmers with goods to sell. In Nicaragua, in Central America, the government has laid special emphasis on the building of trunk highways into isolated farm areas, and then building "neighborhood roads" to give the local farmers access to these highways. Other countries have taken similar action to meet this problem, though on the whole, probably not enough attention has been paid to it.

COLONIZATION

Finally, there is need in many countries to open up new lands to the farmer. In many cases lands currently in use are overcrowded, while there are extensive areas that could be opened up to farmers who are anxious to get land of their own. In some instances, the mere opening of highways and lateral roads is sufficient to bring new lands into use and make it possible to move farmers from overcrowded areas onto them. The Central American Republic of Guatemala has found this to be the case. However, in other instances, the opening up of new areas involves a considerable amount of additional capital investment. Thus, India has found it necessary not only to develop large irrigation projects but also to spend a good deal of money on the acquisition of machinery to root out destructive grasses from areas that once were good farmlands, and to open up entirely new crop areas in the jungle regions.

Some countries have special problems in this regard. For instance, the republics in the archipelagoes of the Philippines and Indonesia find that one of the islands (Luzon in the case of the former and Java in the latter instance) is severely overcrowded, while others are underpopulated. For them the main problem is one of transporting population from the overcrowded areas to the ones in need of inhabitants. This involves a considerable expenditure of money in order to open up new lands in the islands to which population is to be transferred, to finance the farmers there until their crops can come in, and to assure the newly settled farmers transportation facilities to get their crops to market.

Any program involving transfer of populations from one part of a country to another will undoubtedly run into cultural and psychological barriers. Rural populations that have been resident in one area for many generations often have developed a very strong attachment to that area, which may be reinforced by religious or superstitious factors. Indonesia has encountered this difficulty in trying to get the Javanese to move from their home island to the "outer islands." The government has found that the best method is to move whole villages, and to try to reestablish in the new area a village that is as much as possible like that from which the people came.

The Republic of Bolivia in South America has run into similar problems in trying to get the Indians from the highlands of the country to move down into the extraordinarily rich lands of the eastern part of the country. The climatic differences of the areas are exceedingly great; the Indians are not accustomed to growing the kinds of products that will flourish in the lowlands of the east, and they have, in any case, a tremendous attachment to the bleak plateau on which they and their ancestors have lived for hundreds and perhaps thousands of years.

SUMMARY

Hence, in the case of agriculture, as in other aspects of a development program, many factors must be taken into consideration. There is need for education, for arousing incentive, for an adequate credit system, for heavy capital investment. However, developing nations will find in the long run that their whole economic development program will make more rapid progress if they do not forget about the agricultural part of their economy, if they will allocate some of the technical training, funds, and capital equipment of their general program to the needs of agriculture.

6

Problems of Raising Capital in Underdeveloped Countries

Economic development and industrialization require vast amounts of capital. A great deal of investment is needed in order to build factories, construct power plants, extend transportation facilities, and provide the vast amount of social capital in the form of schools, hospitals, public health services, and the like, which a modern industrial nation requires. Obtaining this capital is one of the hardest problems the developing countries must solve.

Before proceeding to explore the question of where the underdeveloped countries can obtain from within their own borders the resources to accumulate this necessary capital equipment, it is worth while to note that in one way at least the present underdeveloped countries have an advantage over the nations that industrialized earlier. Great Britain, the first industrial country, had to begin her manufacturing career with very primitive machinery, because it was all that had been invented up to that time. Slowly, her engineers, inventors, and manufacturers developed more complicated and more economical machines, and these were put to work in British factories. In a word, Great Britain and other countries that pioneered modern industry had to go through the whole process of the growth of the factory from little more than a workshop to the modern assembly plant.

The presently developing countries are in the fortunate position of being able to jump over many of the stages of capital development that Britain and other early industrial powers had to undergo. The countries of Asia, Africa, and Latin America can bring into use immediately machines that represent the experience and knowledge accumulated in two centuries of the Industrial Revolution.

NEED FOR CAPITAL

However, regardless of this advantage, the problem remains of where the underdeveloped countries are going to get the resources to acquire these modern capital goods. Insofar as capital is raised from sources within the developing country, the problem is easily stated, though it is difficult to resolve. The basic need is to divert some of the income of the pre-industrial society into investment channels; or, to put it another way, to transfer some of the labor and goods currently being used for other purposes to the task of building up the stock of capital equipment.*

* It is important to note that the diversion of *goods* from current use to the accumulation of capital is much more painful for the

In an already industrialized nation this task is comparatively easy. It is achieved by channeling the savings of those large segments of the population that have some income left over after meeting their everyday needs, and devoting these savings to investment. One might suppose that the same procedure could be used in the underdeveloped nations. However, in practice this proves very difficult and sometimes almost impossible.

Before there can be the kind of heavy investment required by a development and industrialization program, there must be savings. Some part of the nation's current income must be put aside and not spent for consumption goods or for current commercial or agricultural purposes. However, in the underdeveloped countries there is, almost by definition, widespread poverty. The great mass of the people do not receive sufficient income to allow them to afford a decent living, let alone put any of their income aside in the form of savings. Only a very small group in the upper classes are potential savers and hence potential investors in industrial enterprises.

However, even among the small groups of comparatively wealthy individuals, the "spirit of enterprise" that is supposed to be the basis of economic growth and development is not so widespread as the people in the already developed nations might expect it to be. The richer classes maintain their social

---

underdeveloped nation than the diversion of labor. As we have noted in Chapter Two, most underdeveloped countries suffer from under-employment; that is, they do not have enough work available to keep them fully occupied. Hence, the same amount of work could be done —and probably be done more efficiently—by less people than are now employed in doing it. Thus, the diversion of underemployed people into new industries in many cases will not in fact result in a smaller amount of production in agriculture, the old artisan crafts, and commerce.

position in part by what Thorstein Veblen called "conspicuous consumption," which involves spending on current living expenses virtually everything they receive in income. Furthermore, these classes feel that their superior social status is closely tied up with their continuance in their traditional occupations. Finally, manufacturing industry is new and strange, and therefore unattractive, to those groups that might be expected to take the initiative in developing it.

INADEQUACY OF SAVINGS GROUPS

In most underdeveloped countries there are four principal groups that might logically be expected to be savers—that is, who receive incomes sufficiently large to meet their needs and to have a little bit left over. These are the landlord class, the merchant class, those people associated with the higher ranks of government, and finally the professional classes—lawyers, doctors, and so on. However, although these groups are relatively well-to-do, they have not, by and large, been able or anxious to invest in industry or other aspects of an economic development program.

The landlord class not only is not generally interested in investment in industry, but feels that to be associated with manufacturing is socially degrading. In addition, semifeudal and castelike traditions make the rural landowner tend to spend all the income he receives. When he does save, he is likely to put his savings into more land rather than into something like industry with which he has no experience and of which he is suspicious.

The merchants are somewhat more receptive to the idea of investing in industry, and as we shall see, in some countries have played an important role in the establishment of manufacturing enterprises. However, they too are frequently unwilling to risk their available funds in manufacturing. Most merchants in underdeveloped countries are used to doing business on the basis of a very large profit margin and a very quick turnover. They are anxious to handle goods that will be taken from their shelves in the quickest time possible. They are not likely to be attracted by the prospect of a factory, which is a gamble at best, and which will take a considerable amount of time to establish and may not make profits for some time after it is in operation.

High government officials, another group with higher-than-average incomes in the underdeveloped countries, are even less likely than the landowners and merchants to invest in industry, at least in its early days. More often than not, under-developed nations are characterized by political instability. As a result, those who are today in government positions of importance have no assurance that they will hold those posts tomorrow, or even that they will still be in the country. There are thus two tendencies evident on the part of government officials. First, they seek to get as much wealth as possible as quickly as possible. Second, they tend to put that wealth in forms that will not be easily destroyed or confiscated if they should fall from power.

As a result, the government officials of the underdeveloped nations are probably the single largest group responsible for one of the peculiar phenomena of those nations—the export of capital. Although capital is scarce in the underdeveloped nations, and they remain underdeveloped in part for that reason, most of these nations are exporters of sizable amounts of capital. Their citizens have more or less large accounts in United States, British, or Swiss banks; they own real estate in Miami or on the Riviera; they own foreign bonds or shares in foreign corporations.

Certainly, the last thing in which a politician in an unstable situation would be likely to invest would be manufacturing industry in his own country. Aside from his lack of familiarity with this type of enterprise—which he shares with the land-owning class and the merchants—the politician would be fearful of the possibility of losing his property or seeing it destroyed as a result of the next change of government. If he is going to invest inside his own country at all, he will put his funds in rural land, or in urban real estate, where the return on his investment will be sure and rapid.

Indeed, all the wealthy groups in the underdeveloped nations are likely to invest heavily in urban real estate once the development process has got under way. The rapid growth of the cities makes such speculative investment particularly inviting, and large funds that one might expect to find their way into manufacturing industry are invested in the construction of office buildings or middle- and upper-class housing developments.

The professional classes are the fourth group in the underdeveloped countries with better-than-average incomes. Perhaps before the process of economic development gets fairly under way it would be difficult to separate them from the other three classes. The doctors, lawyers, dentists, engineers, and other professionals will in all likelihood be recruited from the families of the landlords, merchants, or government officials.

However, once economic development begins to gain some momentum, the professional people begin to stand out more clearly as a middle-class group apart from the agrarian and mercantile aristocracy, and they begin to play a significant role in the growth of industry. Engineers in particular are likely to be managers of industrial enterprises. The professional classes in general tend to be somewhat more venturesome than the other three classes. In Brazil, Argentina, and Chile the author found that professional people were among the best customers for stocks of industrial corporations.

SOURCES OF CAPITAL

Some studies have been made of the sources of industrial capital in the developing nations of Latin America. The present author, for example, has made a cursory survey of the situation in Argentina, Brazil, and Chile. He found a surprisingly uniform pattern in those three countries. The great majority of manufacturing firms in all three nations were begun by artisans, many of them immigrants from Europe. Shoemakers, weavers, metalworkers, and other craftsmen set up small shops to serve a very local market. They lived abstemiously, and reinvested their earnings in their businesses. Their workshops thus grew from strictly family enterprises into firms employing workers from outside the family. As time went on and the market grew, these workshops became small factories, and the small factories became larger. In some cases these one-time artisans' workshops became huge manufacturing concerns, doing millions of dollars of business a year.

A secondary source of capital in Argentina, Brazil, and Chile was found to be the merchant class. Some merchants turned to the production of some of the goods they were selling. Perhaps the outstanding example of this method of establishing a manufacturing enterprise is that of the Matarazzo firm in Brazil. Francisco Matarazzo, a poor Italian immigrant, started his career as an itinerant peddler, selling his wares in the backlands of the State of São Paulo. After a while he began to manufacture his own lard, one of the products he was peddling. From that first "manufacturing enterprise" there grew up an empire that includes metallurgy, textiles, canning, construction, and a wide range of other activities.

Professor Sanford Mosk, of the University of California, has made a study of the growth of manufacturing in Mexico. He discovered that the "old industrialists" of that republic were principally large merchants who added small workshops to their commercial establishments in order to produce some of the wares they were selling. Beginning in the 1920's and 1930's a "new industrial class" composed of the "Socialist millionaires"—the generals, colonels, and others who had made their fortunes during the turbulent days of the Mexican Revolution—came into existence. They are the ones who have given impetus to the particularly rapid development of Mexican manufacturing since 1940.

Once the industrialization process has begun and a class of manufacturing entrepreneurs has come into existence, it is this group itself that does the lion's share of the private investing in industry. An entrepreneur who has started in one particular field will be likely to branch out into another related industry. Groups of manufacturers will join to set up enterprises that are too big for any one of them to undertake.

It is the author's observation that the industrial entrepreneurs are the group in the underdeveloped nations that fit most closely the classical economist's concept of businessmen. These are the people who have a sense of thrift, who are conscious savers—albeit living well themselves. These are the people who have some concept of what is meant by efficiency in production. These are the people who are willing to take risks. It is not until such a class has come into existence that any great reliance can be put upon the forces of "private enterprise" as the motive force for economic growth and development.

The growth of industry from small workshops and commercial establishments is a slow and painful process of trial and error. Most of the underdeveloped nations do not have the time to allow this "natural" process to work itself out. Indeed, Dr. Gunnar Myrdal has suggested that if the underdeveloped countries were to depend only on such processes they probably never would develop at all, since the rapid advances of the already developed countries would make it virtually impossible for the crude industries of the underdeveloped nations to meet competition.

In any case, whether or not the underdeveloped countries could develop manufacturing by this process of what Karl Marx called "primitive accumulation" is largely an academic question. The fact is that the underdeveloped countries are eager to progress rapidly, and are not willing to wait the decades or perhaps centuries that the "natural" process of growth would make necessary. As a result, the underdeveloped countries have almost universally resorted to government action to speed up the process of industrialization.

FORCED SAVINGS

The governments of the underdeveloped countries seek to speed up the process of development by bringing about "forced savings" and then taking these savings and investing them in the capital goods—the highways, telegraph and telephone systems, hydroelectric projects, steel mills, and factories that are part and parcel of economic development. These governments can theoretically force the people of their countries to save more than they might otherwise do by two methods: by taxation and by inflation. In practice, the latter method is used more frequently than the former.

93

Taxation is by all odds the more difficult method for governments of underdeveloped countries to use in raising necessary funds for economic development. First of all, the old wealthy classes—the landlords and merchants—remain politically very strong, in most cases strong enough to prevent themselves from being heavily taxed. In the second place, if a government were to try to raise needed revenue by increasing sales and excise taxes, this would immediately engender such unpopularity among the masses of the voters that it could not long remain in office.

Finally, the fact is that people in the underdeveloped countries are not used to paying direct taxes. Great Britain, the United States, and a handful of other nations are exceptions in this world insofar as the payment of income taxes and similar levies are concerned. People in the underdeveloped nations —and even in a highly developed nation like France—find it very hard to understand why citizens of the Anglo-Saxon nations are willing more or less voluntarily to report their income to the government each year, and docilely pay the required taxes thereupon. An attempt to rely principally on income taxes for the government revenue necessary for development—even if it were politically possible to get such tax legislation enacted—might well result in many countries in the government's spending a very large portion of its income-tax revenue on the process of collecting the tax.

INFLATION

Although taxes may provide part of the funds the governments wish to spend on economic development, inflation generally proves to be a much easier source of these funds. Hence, the governments of many underdeveloped nations proceed to spend considerably more than they take in taxes, generally by borrowing enough from their respective central banks to cover their deficits.

The effect of this deficit financing by the government of the underdeveloped nations is to have the government go out into the market and compete with its funds—or make it possible for others to compete with funds supplied by the government—for the materials and labor needed for economic development projects. The result of this increased competition is to raise the prices of these commodities. As the prices of production goods and services go up, so do the prices of other things sold in the country, thus resulting in an almost continuous inflation.

Economists in the highly developed nations generally tend to look upon inflation as a more or less unbridled evil. Insofar as the underdeveloped nations are concerned, such is certainly not the case, however. The whole matter depends upon what the objective of the government of the underdeveloped nations is, and what means it has available for obtaining this objective. If the objective is economic development, if it is not feasible to resort to sufficient taxation, and if it is impossible to supplement tax revenues enough by loans or other aid from outside the nation, then deficit financing and the inflation it brings in its train is the only possible alternative.

If one is to abolish inflation completely in the underdeveloped countries, this means that economic development must be halted, or it must be held to the labored pace made possible by tax revenue and such foreign aid as can be borrowed or begged. At the present moment it is virtually impossible in most countries to have rapid economic development without inflation.

Of course, what financing economic development through inflation means in fact is that the funds and resources for industrialization and other necessary projects are taken largely from the part of the population that falls within the *lower money income* brackets. The rural laborer, sharecropper, or semifeudal tenant pays little of these costs, since he gets little or no money income in any case. The very wealthy pay considerably less than their share, since they are paying in proportion to their purchases but not in accordance with their ability to pay—that is, they pay higher prices than they would otherwise for the things they buy, but the proportion of their income they pay does not increase (as in the case of a progressive income tax) with the amount of their income.

It is thus the urban worker who earns a money income, the small merchant, the craftsman, and those rural workers who labor for a wage who bear the brunt of the cost of economic development if such development is financed by inflation. They are the ones who spend all or most of the income they receive. They are the ones whom an increase in price hurts most.

This is not a socially just situation. This is not the situation that would be preferred by most of those in the underdeveloped countries who urge industrialization. Indeed, most of the advocates of economic development in the underdeveloped nations undoubtedly are not aware of the fact that what they are advocating is in fact paid for in this manner. However, given the institutional and political realities in most of the underdeveloped nations, there would seem to be little alternative to having much of the burden of inflation borne by these lower-income groups, and to having much of the cost of economic development financed by inflation.

USES OF GOVERNMENT FUNDS

With the funds the governments raise, they proceed to the job of economic development. This job can be tackled through two basic mechanisms. The government itself can directly set up the industry or service it desires to see established, or it can provide funds for private individuals or companies who are willing to undertake the task.

The governments of the underdeveloped nations are most likely to undertake direct investment themselves in providing general public utilities. Thus, governments frequently build railroads, electric-light and power grids, large irrigation projects, and new port facilities. They also frequently invest in the heavier type of industry, such as petroleum production and refining, and iron and steel manufacturing. More often than not such direct investment by the government is administered through a wholly or largely government-owned autonomous corporation, but the control as well as the financing of the enterprise remains in government hands.

In addition to these directly state-controlled investments, the governments of many developing nations have established banking institutions to aid the process of economic development by lending to and otherwise investing in private enterprises. These government banks have included central banks as well as special development banks or corporations. These institutions are necessary not only because of the general scarcity of capital and the relatively limited ability of the government to obtain it, but also because the banking systems of most of the underdeveloped countries are inadequate to the task of giving extensive aid to economic development.

In the developing countries that until recently have had almost completely agricultural, pastoral, or mining economies, the banking system has been designed principally to serve these interests and the trade arising from them. The banks of the underdeveloped nations have concerned themselves mainly with the task of financing the principal mineral or agricultural exports and of the imports arising from them. In some countries the banks have also helped to finance the large landholders' crops. In recent years they have tended to extend their activities to financing investment in urban real estate; but seldom have the traditional banking systems of the underdeveloped countries been willing to go beyond this to extend credit to new industries. Investment banking houses, which in the already developed nations carry the principal burden of purchasing new stock issued by companies and reselling it to the general public, have been all but nonexistent.

The reasons for the traditional banking systems not being interested in the problems of economic development are fairly simple. In many cases these banking institutions are branches or subsidiaries of banks in the already developed countries. They have been established principally for the purpose of aiding firms in the older industrial nations to obtain the raw materials and foodstuff they need in the underdeveloped nations. They have been more in the nature of service institutions for the already developed countries than integral parts of the economies of the countries in which they are doing business. Even those private banks that have been developed by nationals of the underdeveloped nations have tended to follow the pattern set by their older foreign confreres.

CENTRAL BANKS IN UNDERDEVELOPED NATIONS

As a result of this inadequacy of the traditional banking systems, the governments of many of the underdeveloped countries have found themselves forced to establish other banking institutions to serve the specific needs of economic development. The cornerstones of these new banking structures have been the central banks of the various underdeveloped nations.

A central bank is a bankers' bank and an agent of the government in carrying out its economic and financial policies. Some of the functions of the central bank of any country are to back up the private lending institutions of the country in case they are in temporary difficulties, to supervise them, to see to it that they do not get into difficulties, and to act as a depository for the excess funds of the private banks. In countries that have government controls over foreign exchange, the central bank is usually the institution that administers these controls. Finally, the central bank is usually the place where the government keeps its funds, is generally the only institution empowered by law to issue bank notes, and is the principal organization to which the government turns when it wants to borrow funds. This last process is accomplished by the government selling its bonds to the central bank in return for which the bank opens an account in favor of the government, upon which the government can then draw checks to pay its bills.

Most of the countries of Latin America established central banks in the 1920's and 1930's, although a few countries, including Cuba, Haiti, and the Dominican Republic, did so only in the years immediately following the Second World War.

In the countries of Asia and Africa that have achieved their independence since the war, one of the first acts of economic policy has been either to establish a central bank or to name an existing institution to engage in the functions of a central bank.

DEVELOPMENT BANKS

In addition to central banks, most governments of developing nations have established special development banks and institutions. In some cases these have been specialized organizations, extending credit only to industry or only to agriculture, while in other instances they have been more general in nature.

One of the earliest and most famous of these institutions is the Chilean Development Corporation. It has not only financed direct government investments in the petroleum and steel industries and in hydroelectric power but has also extended a great variety of help to a wide range of private businesses. The corporation has used many methods to extend such help. In some cases it has provided capital by helping to reorganize existing private firms, and buying stock in them. In other instances it has helped to bring new firms into existence by buying a sizable part of the original capital stock in them. On still other occasions it has bought bonds of existing or new corporations. Finally, it has extended short- and medium-term credit to some enterprises.

The Chilean Development Corporation has helped many different manufacturing enterprises. These include firms in the metallurgical field, pharmaceutical companies, oil refineries, cement plants, clothing firms, and a wide variety of other industrial enterprises.

Most of the other countries of Latin America have established development institutions more or less similar to the Chilean Development Corporation. The new countries of Asia and Africa have done likewise. They have all felt the need for direct government help to get new industries established and to aid the expansion of old ones.

From what has gone before, it is obvious that the almost unanimous action of the governments of the underdeveloped countries in investing directly in the process of industrialization and economic growth has been the result of necessity rather than any ideological predilection on the part of these regimes. The self-styled Socialist governments of India and Ghana have followed the same policy as the conservative governments of Brazil and Chile and the totalitarian government of Perón's Argentina.

CONCLUSION

The governments of the underdeveloped countries have realized, regardless of their ideological bent, that if economic development was to be carried out rapidly, this could only be accomplished by the direct intervention of the government in the process. Only the governments of these countries were capable, through taxation and deficit spending, of mobilizing the resources necessary to carry forward with dispatch the process of industrialization, and the construction of transportation, communication, and power facilities to serve new manufacturing industries.*

---

* On June 24, 1958, the New York *Times* quoted President Juscelino Kubitschek of Brazil (an essentially conservative statesman) as saying that the governments of the underdeveloped countries must take the lead in industrialization, not out of "ideological preference" or a

"deliberate tendency toward statism" but as a "simple imperative of circumstances." The *Times*' article paraphrases Kubitschek as saying that "underdeveloped countries citizens' savings were not sufficient to create national investment capital, while international lending institutions lacked sufficient resources and were limited by their own statutes. . . . He said that, since private capital was not attracted by risky undertakings where earnings are low, the Government must move in to pave the way."

7

Problems of Foreign Investment in the Developing Countries

United States Secretary of the Treasury George Humphrey led his country's delegation to the Inter-American Economic Conference held in Rio de Janeiro in October 1955. He delivered a now famous speech at that conference in which he got off his chest what he thought was good advice to the underdeveloped nations of the new world. Summed up, this advice was to stop asking Uncle Sam for handouts, to realize the fact that they were going to have to carry the greater part of the burden of their own economic development, and that the only "aid" they could expect to get from the United States was in the form of private foreign investment in profitable enterprises within their borders. If they wanted to get such investment, he said, they had better set their houses in such order that North American businessmen would find it profitable to invest in the countries south of the Rio Grande.

Had it not been for the innate politeness of the Latin American, the natural caution of the diplomats who made up most of the delegations present, and the need of the Latin Americans not to antagonize the United States too much, this speech would have caused a scandal in the Rio de Janeiro Conference. It did cause a scandal in the Latin American press. Yet Mr. Humphrey was expressing a point of view that is still widely held in the industrialized countries, and particularly in the United States. It is still very generally believed in those countries that most of the help for the development of the less advanced countries must come through the traditional channels of business—by citizens of the developed nations buying bonds of the governments and enterprises of the less advanced countries, and by firms of the industrialized countries extending their operations to the unindustrialized states. This belief is bulwarked by a sneaking conviction that somehow or other this is the only decent and honorable way for the great industrial powers to help their less fortunate neighbors.

However, the peoples of the underdeveloped nations see the problem from an entirely different focus. They have had a certain amount of experience already with private foreign investment. They have strong reasons to be skeptical of it as final answer to the problem of foreign aid to their economies. They are also more aware than are many people in the highly industrialized countries that even with the best will in the world on the part of the developing nations, private foreign investment cannot adequately do the job that needs doing.

USEFULNESS OF FOREIGN INVESTMENT

The basic argument in favor of receiving private foreign investment for the process of economic development is a simple one. The unindustrialized nations are, for the most part, exceedingly poor. For them to divert sizable portions of their current income to the building of transport systems, power projects, and factories is exceedingly painful because it involves, for the time being at least, reducing still further the already very low purchasing power of large groups of their citizens.

Insofar as the underdeveloped nations can acquire help from abroad, it becomes unnecessary to divert income from current uses and thus impose hardship on the people. In effect, when the citizens of a highly industrialized country establish a factory, for example, in an underdeveloped nation, the unindustrialized country is receiving a "loan" of that factory. It does not have to put aside immediately sufficient income to pay for it. It receives it without any reduction of current expenditures, and pays back the cost of the equipment out of future income. Insofar as the foreign capital is productively used, the factory itself will increase the total national income sufficiently that the investment can be paid back out of this increase. Other things being equal, therefore, foreign investment in an unindustrialized country makes that country's industrialization less painful to its citizenry.

Foreign investment has other advantages. Firms coming in from abroad bring with them technicians who know all the latest methods used in the already industrialized countries. The underdeveloped nation, therefore, does not have to wait until it has trained its own corps of engineers and technicians to be able to make use of these techniques.

105

Furthermore, a foreign firm will probably bring into the underdeveloped nation the same kind of up-to-date machinery being used in its plants at home. It will also make available to its subsidiary the patents and other advantages it possesses in the home country, and the subsidiary will have the added benefit to the underdeveloped country that it can make full use of the research and development programs of the home company. Thus, the technical improvements and innovations made in the highly industrialized nation can quickly be passed on to the underdeveloped country.

In the light of these advantages of foreign investment, many people in the already industrialized nations find it difficult to understand why there is any resistance at all to foreign investment in the underdeveloped nations. Particularly is this so, in view of the fact that the developing countries have already received a considerable impetus in their development from foreign-owned firms. Many of the mines, the railroad systems, the telephone and telegraph networks, the large-scale agricultural enterprises, as well as the early factories, were built by private foreign companies. The unindustrialized nations thus got their first impetus toward development from this type of help from abroad.

OPPOSITION TO FOREIGN INVESTMENT

From whence comes opposition to foreign investment, then? The answer to this question is a complicated one. It involves improper behavior by many of the early foreign investors and resentment at seeing the unindustrialized country's resources developed for the benefit of the large industrial powers rather than for the national welfare of the underdeveloped country. It also stems from fear of tying the economy of the developing country too close to that of a large industrialized power. There is also concern about the burden of debt upon which interest and dividends must be paid for a long time in the future. Finally, the development of nationalism in the underdeveloped nations has made all these fears, resentments, and jealousies particularly acute.

There is little doubt that there is a dark side to the history of foreign investment in the unindustrialized nations. Most of the colonial empires built up in the nineteenth century came into being when political control followed—or sometimes preceded—the commerce of the great industrial powers. British penetration of India, for example, was first undertaken by the English East India Company, which established trading posts at various points in the subcontinent, garrisoned these trading centers, and then spread its control from there into neighboring areas until the company had control of the whole of modern India and Pakistan. Only in 1857 did the British government officially take over the government of India.

A similar story can be found in the case of the partition of Africa. Trade, or the hope for trade, as well as strategical considerations and national rivalries among the great industrial nations, explain the division of the once Dark Continent among the principal European countries.

Even those areas, such as Latin America, in which the political sovereignty of the various nations remained more or less intact were characterized by the same type of economic penetration followed by vast political influence. Loans were made during the latter part of the nineteenth century and the beginning of the twentieth by the European powers and the United States to the Latin American nations, as were direct investments in banking, railroads, mining, and agricultural enterprises. On the excuse of collecting these loans and protecting these investments, German warships imposed their will on Venezuela, the British engaged in "gunboat diplomacy" with several Latin American countries, and United States Marines occupied Nicaragua, Panama, the Dominican Republic, Haiti, and Cuba at one time or another. Even in some of the Latin American countries that suffered relatively little military intervention by one of the big powers, such as Brazil, Argentina, Uruguay, and Chile, there was a widespread feeling—which was to a large degree probably true—that their governments were more often subject to pressures from foreign governments than from their own electorates.

Many of the early foreign firms that operated in the underdeveloped countries quite unabashedly took a hand in local politics. They used campaign contributions, good jobs, outright bribery, threats of foreign intervention, and other means to influence the selection and policies of governments. In colonial countries firms from the "mother country" had the ear of the colonial governments directly.

Furthermore, many of the early foreign investors received excessive favors. To a considerable degree some special concessions were probably inevitable in order to get foreign firms to take the risks of establishing new enterprises in these nations. However, there is no doubt that many of the concessions granting exemption from taxes, subsidies for building railroads, and other privileges that were not granted to citizens of these countries came to be resented. Although many of these concessions may not have grated against national feeling in the last decades of the nineteenth century, they certainly did so by the third or fourth decade of the present one.

Even apart from political intervention and special privileges, the early foreign concerns in the underdeveloped countries often came to be resented for the simple reason that they tended to be bigger than the local government itself. The

United Fruit Company in the central American republics and the Unilever interests in the countries of West Africa are two examples of such overshadowing firms. Their mere size relative to the nations in which they operated made them targets for dislike and distrust, as local nationalism began to develop strongly.

The early labor policies of many of the foreign firms also aroused a great deal of resentment, some of which still lingers, though generally such policies are long since a thing of the past. The payment of low wages, strong resistance to trade unionism, and a general attitude of treating their workers like children even after they had "grown up," so to speak, developed deep resentments in the underdeveloped countries.

The behavior of many of the Europeans and United States citizens working for the foreign firms in the underdeveloped countries in the days before the Great Depression of the 1930's also helped to develop deep suspicions of private foreign investors. These foreign employees tended to form a class apart in the mines, transportation facilities, or other enterprises in which they worked. They had much better housing than even local employees of similar social status; they had their own clubs, their own schools, their own hospitals, all of which were generally better than similar facilities for local employees. Although generally these policies are also a thing of the past, memories of them linger on.

The rise of nationalism has resulted in the development of other grounds for opposition to private foreign companies in the underdeveloped countries. There has grown up a widespread feeling that the foreign firms that have opened up mines, transport facilities, and other enterprises have done so for the purpose of serving the highly industrialized countries from which these firms came rather than for the benefit of the underdeveloped countries themselves. Mines were opened because the United States or the western European countries needed the ore; transport facilities were developed in order to get mineral or agricultural products to European or United States markets.

Those who present this argument in the unindustrialized nations maintain that there have been at least two results stemming from this situation. In the first place, this has often made for very lopsided and peculiarly organized economies. For instance, in Peru it was only in recent years that a national railway network was developed, because the early railways ran from the mines to the nearest port, while the principal cities of the country remained unconnected. In Argentina the same phenomenon has resulted in the strange system whereby to get between two cities in the interior that are a few score miles from each other, one must go several hundred miles back toward the grain ports of Buenos Aires or Rosario, and return on another rail line, no direct connections having been constructed among many of the towns of the interior.

The second argument is that the foreign companies, in the case of mining in particular, have exploited the resources of the underdeveloped country without any consideration for the possible future development of that nation. Once mineral resources are gone they cannot be replaced, and the argument is often heard that the minerals of some of the underdeveloped nations may well be exhausted before they can be put to use in building up the economies of these nations themselves. The resources will be gone, and little will have been left to the underdeveloped nation in return for their disappearance.

Growing nationalism, as well as increasing consciousness of the dangers of depression and unemployment, has engendered another argument against foreign investment of the old type: fear of tying the underdeveloped nation's economy too closely to that of one of the big industrial powers. There exist both fear of the exercise of political pressure, as the result of large economic influence of an industrial power in an unindustrialized nation, and fear that economic crises in the already developed countries will be passed on to the economically less advanced nations.

There is also fear that foreign investment of the old style will result in the piling up of a burden of debt that will be hard for the underdeveloped nation to sustain. Interest must be paid on bonds held by foreigners, and dividends must go to stockholders of foreign-owned firms. Both interest and dividends must come from the underdeveloped nation's limited supply of foreign currency earned by that country. As more investments are made, the larger will be the amount of dividends and interest that the underdeveloped nation will have to pay each year to the industrialized power. Less and less foreign currency will be available therefore to pay for imports of consumption goods and new capital equipment.

Finally, with the growth of greater national self-consciousness in the underdeveloped countries, there has evolved a widespread conviction that the basic industries of these countries should be in the hands of their own nationals. Hence, there is increasing unwillingness to allow private foreign firms to invest in railroads, power plants, and in some cases even in petroleum and mining.

LACK OF FOREIGN INVESTMENT RESOURCES

All these arguments serve to explain the reservations many people in the underdeveloped nations feel about allowing further large-scale private foreign investment in many fields.

However, in addition to these there is another fundamental fact that serves to limit the role of private foreign investors in economic development of the presently less advanced nations. This is the unavailability of sufficient private capital to do the job even if the underdeveloped nations were willing to have private investors try to do it.

The highly industrialized nations themselves are going through significant technological changes that call for heavy capital investment. Most private capital funds, therefore, will find profitable outlets at home. The development of new industries, such as electronics, atomic energy, synthetics, the spread of automation, the expansion and rebuilding of cities, and other phenomena will tie up most private capital resources in still further developing the already advanced nations. Experience since the Second World War has demonstrated that except for the petroleum industry, and to a much less degree manufacturing, there has been relatively little export of private capital by the advanced nations to the less advanced ones. There is no indication that this situation is likely to change in the near future.

Hence private capital from the more advanced countries is unable to bear more than a small part of the burden of development in the less advanced nations. Generally speaking, the underdeveloped countries are willing to accept a certain degree of foreign private investment. Thirty years ago, Victor Raúl Haya de la Torre, the great Peruvian politician and one of the earliest serious students of this problem in the underdeveloped nations, stated the position that is widely held in Latin America and in other areas of developing economies today. Haya said:

". . . we consider that foreign capital is necessary in a country of limited economic development such as ours. But it is also necessary to remember that the lack of scientific economic knowledge in this country has made possible the acceptance of the belief that it is necessary to accept foreign capital from wherever it comes and in whatever way it may come. This is an error. Those who argue that to control foreign capital is to frighten it away forget an economic law: the law of the expansion of capital, which forces it to balance these two forces . . . we shall be able to live in good relations with foreign capital, without becoming dependent on it; defending thus the stability of our own economy and making of foreign capital a cooperating element for national economic development." *

CONDITIONS FOR FOREIGN INVESTMENT

The underdeveloped nations are today establishing the conditions under which foreign private capital is welcome within their borders. In general these conditions are:

1. Foreign enterprises must obey the laws of the country in which they are operating, particularly the labor and social laws and tax statutes.

2. Foreign firms must operate on the basis of equality with native enterprises, expecting no special privileges and being the victims of no discriminatory practices. They must not appeal to their home governments so long as they are being treated on a par with national firms.

3. Foreign companies must as quickly as possible become "national" by bringing local investors into partnership in the enterprises, by using as many local people as possible in managerial and other responsible posts, by using as large a percentage of local raw materials as feasible.

* *Politica Aprista* (Lima, 1933), p. 59.

4. Foreign investments must come into areas of the economy where they are welcome, and come principally to serve the interests of the nation in which they operate rather than those of the country from which they come.

5. Foreign firms must stay out of local politics.

6. Foreign companies must be moderate in the demands they make on the local supply of foreign currency. Thus, over and above a certain agreed percentage of profit that they can take out in foreign exchange, they must reinvest their profits in the country in which they are operating; and they must not attempt to repatriate their investments too rapidly.

Although few if any of the underdeveloped nations have stated the terms on which they will accept foreign private investments as specifically as we have done, there is a general tendency to adopt these criteria. Some nations do not feel themselves strong enough to insist on all of these conditions; some do not feel the necessity to do so; but virtually all tend to operate to a greater or lesser degree on the basis of the conditions we have set forth.

It is the author's observation that most of those companies in the highly industrialized nations (or at least in the United States) that are interested in investing in the underdeveloped countries are willing to abide by reasonable rules and conditions. Their fundamental purposes in going abroad are two in number—to make a profit and to add to the prestige of the firm and those running it by having holdings in another country. If the rules established by the countries in which they invest allow them to make a reasonable profit, and do not put them at a disadvantage to other investors, foreign and domestic, they will be willing to abide by these rules. There is a growing awareness among United States businessmen operating in the underdeveloped countries that they are guests and should act as such.

On the other hand, most companies from the industrialized countries will also adapt themselves without protest to a situation in which the rules are lax. If a dictatorship or a corrupt regime is not concerned with the national interests of its country and so does not demand that a foreign firm conform to labor legislation, tax laws, and the like, the foreign companies are not going to insist that they be made to conform. The burden of law enactment and enforcement rests on the governments of the underdeveloped nations, though there is a tendency—perhaps natural under the circumstances—to put the blame on the foreign companies for failure of governments to pass adequate legislation and enforce it, rather than putting the blame upon the local administrations.

FIELDS FOR FOREIGN INVESTMENT

There is no doubt that the field in which private foreign investors are most welcome in the underdeveloped nations is that of manufacturing. The less advanced nations are particularly anxious to establish factory industry. Manufacturing plants can more quickly take on national "protective coloration" than can many other types of firms; they are more obviously designed to serve the local market and hence the interest of the country in which they exist than are many other types of firms.

Some underdeveloped nations have actively sought foreign investment in industry. Thus the West Indian islands of Jamaica, Trinidad, and Puerto Rico, as well as Israel, are among those countries that have a policy of offering freedom from taxes for a specified period of time, as well as other incentives to establish plants within their borders.

Generally there is relatively little opposition in the underdeveloped countries to the establishment of private foreign manufacturing firms within their borders. However, a disquieting note was sounded in April 1958 by a conference of Latin American Socialist parties meeting in Santiago de Chile. They warned against such direct investments as the establishment of factories by foreign firms, alleging that this was a "new type of imperialism" against which the Latin American nations must be especially on their guard. This seems to the author to be an instance of exaggerated nationalism—a kind of cutting off one's nose to spite one's face.

The kind of attitude represented in this statement of the Latin American Socialists high-lights another aspect of the problem of private foreign investment in the underdeveloped countries—the fact that if these countries want to receive the benefits of investment by private foreign firms even on the underdeveloped nations' own terms, they will have to provide an atmosphere conducive to such investment. Undoubtedly, nationalism will have to be kept within reasonable bounds. It does not make sense to argue—as the author has heard some Latin American politicians do—that all foreign capital is somehow dangerous to national sovereignty of the underdeveloped nations but that a failure of foreign firms to invest in these same nations is somehow a huge imperialist plot.

Either foreign firms must be made welcome, and the conditions under which they are welcome must be stated, or the governments and peoples of the underdeveloped nations must make it clear that they do not want any foreign private investment. An attitude of xenophobia and jingoism such as exists in some of the underdeveloped nations, and is fostered by some of their politicians, can only be self-defeating. However, if foreign investments are to be welcomed, it is likely that they can contribute an important although modest part to the growth of the economies of the less advanced nations.

The role of private foreign investment is thus limited by the desires of the underdeveloped nations and the inadequacy of available capital in the economically more advanced countries. It can be expected to bear only a small part of the burden of helping to make the growth of the underdeveloped countries rapid enough so that it can provide a steadily rising standard of living for the people of those nations.

8

"Foreign Aid" and the Problem of Economic Development

The problem of foreign aid for underdeveloped countries looks quite different when viewed from the angle of those nations themselves, and when viewed from the vantage point of the already developed countries. If citizens of the big industrial powers often find it hard to understand the hesitancy of the underdeveloped nations to accept private foreign investment, the people of the unindustrialized countries find it hard to comprehend the reticence of the governments of the highly developed countries about giving them more extensive loans and grants-in-aid.

There is no doubt that the attitude of the people of the less developed countries has considerable validity. Since the role of *private* foreign enterprise in the growth of the economies of the less advanced nations will perforce be limited for reasons we have already discussed, an increasingly large role in this process must be taken by various forms of *public* investment. This fact is insufficiently clear in the already advanced countries. People there tend to continue to think of the whole problem of the development of underdeveloped countries more or less in the context this problem had during the nineteenth century and down to World War I.

BRITAIN AND 19TH CENTURY ECONOMIC DEVELOPMENT

During most of the nineteenth century Great Britain had a virtual monopoly on factory industry. It not only provided most of the world's manufactured goods but also bought most of its raw materials and exported foodstuffs. It also aided considerably the growth of some of the developing nations of that day.

However, Great Britain in the nineteenth century was in a peculiar position that is not occupied by any nation today. It was an island nation, unable or unwilling to grow most of the food its citizens ate. It had few raw materials for industry except coal. Therefore, Great Britain was a tremendously large importer both of foodstuffs and of raw materials. The customers who bought Britain's textiles, metal products, ceramics, even its coal, were able in large part to pay for these by shipping Britain wheat, corn, meat, iron ore, and tropical products, all of which were in great demand in the island kingdom.

The British position was peculiar in other ways. Only a relative handful of countries were "developing nations" then —principally the United States, Germany, and Japan. The last two did not depend upon Great Britain for much help in the industrialization process, which they carried on largely through their respective governments. Hence, the demand on Britain for aid for economic development of other nations was relatively light.

However, there was a sizable group of Britishers who were investors abroad, and they did help considerably in the development of the United States, as well as undertaking the construction of railroads and public utilities in a number of countries of Latin America and Asia (most of the latter being British colonies at the time). British bondholders and stockholders of these enterprises were paid back out of the proceeds from the wheat, cotton, corn, and other products Britain's customers sold to her.

As a result of these circumstances, there never developed a "pound shortage" in the nineteenth century. Britain's need for raw materials and foodstuffs made it possible for those buying British manufactures to pay for most of them through selling Britain other things in return. British investors were willing to put their funds in enterprises abroad, thus providing additional pounds sterling to British customers, and there was a relatively small number of countries actively engaged in developing their economies and depending upon Britain to help them. Hence, the demand for British-manufactured products was seldom very much greater than the amount of pounds sterling Britain's customers had to spend on these products.

THE 20TH CENTURY SITUATION

The situation is fundamentally different in at least three respects in the middle of the twentieth century: the world's great manufacturing nation today is the United States; virtually all those nations of the world that are not yet industrialized are seeking to develop their economies; and (for the time being at least) large amounts of productive resources that might be used to produce capital goods for the underdeveloped nations are being devoted to war and preparation for war on a gigantic scale.

The United States is today the country to which most of the underdeveloped countries of the world turn to get the capital equipment they need. It produces perhaps a third or more of the total world income, and it is by all odds the largest industrial power. It is to the mid-twentieth century what Great Britain was to the nineteenth century.

However, the United States is in a very different situation from that of Great Britain in its heyday. The United States is a continental power, with vast resources of coal, minerals, forests, agricultural raw materials, and foodstuffs. As a result, it is not in Britain's position of needing to buy most of the sinews of its manufacturing industry abroad. Nor does it have to buy most of its food from other countries. Conceivably, the United States could be virtually self-sufficient. Thus, although foreign trade is of some importance—particularly to some industries—it is not basic to our economy in the way that it was to that of Great Britain. The upshot of this is that, unlike Britain, the United States does not make it possible for those countries that want to buy things here to pay for them by selling goods to the United States. There are relatively few things the United States wants from abroad, and they certainly do not compare in bulk or in value to the amount of goods and services other countries would like to buy in the United States if they could acquire the dollars to do so.

The second difference between the United States' position

in the mid-twentieth century and Britain's in the nineteenth is that today what Dr. Gunnar Myrdal calls the Great Awakening has occurred. Virtually all the economically less advanced nations of the world have decided at about the same moment to attempt to develop their economies, and particularly to attempt to industrialize. As a result, there is a tremendous demand for the capital goods of which the United States is the largest producer. The desire for these goods far outruns the ability of the underdeveloped countries to sell goods to the United States in payment for them.

Finally, for almost a generation a large part of the productive capacity of the United States and of most of the other more advanced countries has been taken up with producing goods for war or possible war. Thus the demands of the underdeveloped countries for equipment must compete not only with normal peacetime demands of the developed nations themselves but also with "defense," "rearmament," and similar programs. At the same time, these military programs have provided an outlet for investment by private firms in the highly developed countries, and have made these firms less interested than might otherwise be the case in extensive investment abroad, in the underdeveloped nations.

THE "DOLLAR SHORTAGE"

The net result of all of this was the much discussed "dollar shortage." Many countries, and particularly many underdeveloped countries, sought to purchase much more in the way of both consumers' products and capital equipment from the United States than they could pay for through the sale of goods and services to the United States. Furthermore, only a handful of countries were recipients of enough United States private foreign investment to fill the gap between what they wanted to purchase and the dollars they could earn through sales to the United States.

This situation existed in one form or another for four decades after World War I. During the 1920's large-scale economic development in the less advanced nations had not yet begun, and United States private loans both to the under-developed nations and to the European countries more or less covered the gap and kept the "dollar shortage" from becoming obvious. During the 1930's the situation was met, at least by the more advanced nations, by shipping to the United States most of the world's gold supply in payment for commodities that were not paid for by other goods sold to the United States.

During World War II the handy implement of Lend-Lease was available to meet the situation. The United States virtually gave its friends and Allies the dollars they needed in return for vague promises no one expected would be kept. Subsequent to the war a whole series of stop-gap measures have been adopted. A $5,000,000,000 loan to Britain in 1946, the Marshall Plan program from 1948 to 1952, and various "foreign aid" laws passed by the United States Congress since that time have met the situation on more or less a day-to-day basis.

Two things stand out from all this. First, during the first fifteen years after World War II there was no long-range program (except for a time the Marshall Plan) to seek to coordinate the needs of the United States' customers and the productive capacity of the United States. Second, the chief beneficiaries of these measures to date have been the already developed European countries. The unindustrialized nations have received but a small percentage of the total benefit from these various measures to make dollars available so that other countries could buy the things the United States has available to sell.

Too many economists have not seen clearly the full implications of these recent trends in the world economic situation, particularly since World War II. Some economists have a vast ability to delude themselves—as was amply demonstrated during the Great Depression when by the legion they maintained, in the face of all the evidence around them, that it was impossible to have more goods produced than would be taken off the market and that it was impossible to have large-scale unemployment for any length of time.

At the present time many economists of the already developed nations are as mistaken about the problems of international economic relations as their confreres were a generation ago about the problems of depression and unemployment. They somehow believe that by various panaceas they can avoid coming to grips with what is really the essential problem: the fact that the underdeveloped nations of the world want to buy a great deal more from the United States than can be paid for by United States purchases from abroad.*

THE IMF AND IBRD

For instance, economists of the developed nations worked with the politicians after the Second World War to establish two international organizations which, they hoped, would

---

* It may be argued that the drain on U.S. gold reserves in the late 1950's represents a reversal of the "dollar shortage." However, so far as the underdeveloped nations are concerned, such is not the case. In 1962 it still remains true that these countries have a very large potential demand for U.S. goods and services that is kept from becoming "effective" (that is, expressing itself in actual purchases of these goods and services) only by these nations' inability to sell the U.S. enough to pay for all they would like to buy from this country.

virtually resolve the world's international economic problems: the International Monetary Fund and the International Bank for Reconstruction and Development. It is obvious by now that these organizations as they were originally conceived were entirely inadequate to the task before them.

The International Monetary Fund has as its avowed objective the maintenance of the stability of currencies of the various countries belonging to the fund, and through this the stimulation of trade. Those nations joining the IMF declare upon seeking admission the legal value of their currencies in terms of gold and the United States dollar. They are not allowed to vary this legal value more than 10 per cent without receiving the approval of the fund. They have to deposit with the fund a certain amount of gold or dollars, as well as a certain quantity of their own currency, and these funds are used by the IMF to seek to maintain the stability of one currency with another. A nation that finds itself with a temporary lack of gold or dollars can borrow from the fund, within limits.

The purpose of these arrangements was to establish a system roughly comparable to the gold standard that was dominant during most of the nineteenth century, and with interruptions during the First World War, down to the Great Depression. Under the gold standard all countries stated the value of their currencies in terms of gold, and if they imported more than they exported they settled their accounts by shipments of gold.

However, what the economists who were the authors of the IMF did not take into account was the fact that the situation in the mid-twentieth century was fundamentally different from what it had been in the heyday of the gold standard. The great industrial power of the earlier period, Great Britain, was supplying its customers with most of the pounds sterling they needed by buying large amounts of raw materials and foodstuffs from them and investing in them; and the demands for capital equipment for economic development were relatively small. Thus, there was relatively little likelihood that a country would find itself with a long-sustained, more or less permanent drain on its supply of gold and sterling. However, today the United States is not buying, and is not likely to buy, sufficient goods from abroad to offset the demands for dollars of those underdeveloped countries that would like to buy capital equipment and other products there. Hence, many of these countries today *do* find themselves in a position of constantly wanting to buy more things from the United States than they can sell of their own goods for dollars, and they have a more or less permanent drain on their dollar and gold supply.

The International Monetary Fund arrangement is basically supposed to deal with temporary drains on a country's gold supply and dollars. It is not at all adequate for dealing with the constant and inevitable "dollar shortage" arising from economic development of underdeveloped countries. In fact, there is no institution that *is* designed to handle this long-run problem.

The International Bank for Reconstruction and Development, the other major world economic institution emerging from World War II, was also inadequate for the job it is designed to accomplish. It was supposed to lend funds for development projects on the basis of strict banking principles. Loans were supposed to be more or less self-liquidating, and they were offered at relatively high rates of interest, both of which factors reduced the usefulness of the bank. However, its greatest single limitation was the fact that it did not have sufficient funds really to do the kind of job that needed to be done. At best, the International Bank was a good beginning for the kind of program that is needed.

In recent years it has been found necessary to create subsidiary institutions to the International Bank to deal more realistically with the problems it was supposed to have solved. Thus the International Finance Corporation grants loans with considerably less guarantee of repayment than those of the IBRD itself. The International Development Association grants loans in dollars and other "hard" currencies that can be paid back in the currencies of the developing nations themselves. However, the resources of these IBRD subsidiaries are so far very small, and they and the International Bank itself are still inadequate to the job they are seeking to do.

If the underdeveloped nations are really to be helped effectively in their economic growth, so that they can develop their economies faster than their populations are increasing, a program of considerable variety and flexibility is needed. It is a program calling for efforts on the part of the governments of individual industrialized countries, and of greatly expanded activities by international agencies now in existence or to be created.

TYPES OF FOREIGN AID

There are two basic ways in which help from public sources in the more advanced nations can be made available: through direct extension of aid on a loan or grant basis by governments of more developed nations or by international agencies; and through a program of stabilizing the export income of the underdeveloped countries. The former type of help has been developed on a modest scale since World War II; the latter was for long anathema to many of the highly industrialized countries, particularly the United States.

Since January 1949 when President Harry Truman in his Inaugural Address talked about a "bold new program" to aid the development of the economically less advanced nations, some progress has been made in establishing such programs. The United States has made a world-wide effort of technical assistance ("know-how") and capital aid (funds to purchase machinery, equipment, and so on) that in recent years has generally amounted to about a billion dollars a year. Great Britain has had a smaller program, designed to help principally those countries still part of or formerly part of the British Commonwealth and Empire. France has also had a program of aid to the development of French Africa south of the Sahara; West Germany and a handful of other western European nations have given modest boosts to development in a few nations. The United Nations has had a small technical-aid program, spending less than $100,000,000 a year, and the International Bank has carried out investments on a modest basis. Finally, in very recent years we have seen the Soviet Union enter the field of economic aid, giving loans and some technical aid to those countries in which it has felt the most political capital for the U.S.S.R. was to be acquired. All these efforts amount to only a small fraction of what the underdeveloped nations need. And they have the disadvantage in most cases that they involve a tremendous amount of political bargaining between the developed country and the less advanced country before programs have been approved.

What would be most advantageous to the underdeveloped nations would certainly be some scheme by which all the development efforts of the big industrial powers could be pooled and expanded. Early in 1961 the Kennedy administration did take steps to try to coordinate the program of United States aid to India with those of several of its European Allies and Japan. Later in the year a similar program was worked out for Brazil. However, in the present state of world politics, any general program on the part of all the industrial nations seems highly unlikely for some time to come. The best one can expect, perhaps, is a sizable increase in the programs of each of the individual industrial nations, and a large boost in the development activities of the United Nations.

Increased programs should provide for at least three different types of aid to the underdeveloped nations: loans, grants, and technical assistance. The first two should be designed to meet the fundamental lack of capital in the underdeveloped nations, and the third to overcome the lack of "know-how" there.

There are certainly some projects that might be financed on a loan basis. If a specific development program seems likely either to earn or to save sufficient foreign exchange to pay back its own cost, a loan might well be in order. In other words, if an irrigation project, for instance, was going to permit a country to grow products that hitherto it had had to pay dollars or pounds or some other foreign currency to acquire, it might be the kind of project for which a loan would be indicated.

In order to handle all the loan projects that an amplified program of aid to economic development would imply, the resources of such governmental and intergovernmental lending institutions as the United States Export-Import Bank and the International Bank for Reconstruction and Development will have to be greatly expanded. Lending facilities in the vicinity of fifteen to twenty billion dollars each would certainly seem more appropriate, for a starter, than the present capital of four to six billion that these lending institutions now have to work with.

However, there are large parts of the development programs of the less advanced countries that will never really be self-liquidating. There are many transportation projects, power programs, sewer systems, and other parts of a development program for which it would be very difficult to calculate any appreciable saving of foreign exchange. Of course, educational, hospital, and housing programs are in the same category. For these, nonrepayable grants would be more appropriate.

Such grant-in-aid programs will require vast expansion of the present "foreign aid" programs of the highly industrialized nations such as the United States. They should also provide for the establishment in the United Nations of some agency that will be empowered to make grants instead of loans and that will have enough funds available to do a really significant job.

In this connection the highly developed nations ought to take seriously the suggestion which has been brought up for years in the United Nations by the less economically advanced nations for a Special United Nations Fund for Economic Development (SUNFED). The original proposal for SUNFED involved a planned reduction in armaments expenditures by the major military powers, and the endowment of the UN Special Fund with the funds thus saved. It seems unwise to make the project for economic development of the less advanced countries depend upon the reduction of armaments by the Great Powers. The Special Fund should be established forthwith and be given several billions of dollars to begin its work.

Although disarmament is still in the talking stage, the achievement of a real disarmament agreement among the larger nations would present a new opportunity for the already industrialized nations to aid the development of their less fortunate neighbors. The switching of large expenditures from armaments to economic development, furthermore, would answer a serious problem that is going to face at least some of the industrialized countries. A more or less sudden cessation of armament expenditures, after two decades of them, would make it necessary, for the continued prosperity of the large industrial nations, to have an alternate field for investment. If "peace were to break out," large parts of the economy of the United States and other large nations would be without their customary sources of orders and business. Expenditures on the economic development of the less developed nations could provide such a field.

PRICE STABILIZATION

In addition to providing loans and grants, there is at least one other way in which the economically more advanced nations can assure greater continuity and stability to the programs of development of the less advanced countries. This is through taking measures to assure the market and price for the principal commodities produced by the underdeveloped nations.

The idea of guaranteeing markets and prices for raw materials and foodstuffs is not entirely unfamiliar. Great Britain has assured stability of demand and price for her sugar- and cocoa-growing colonies and former colonies. During the Second World War Great Britain sponsored the establishment in West Africa of a Cocoa Marketing Board, with which the British government then signed five-year contracts for the purchase of the product. This system was continued after the war. In the case of sugar, the British government negotiates periodically with representatives of the British West Indian colonies, establishing quotas in the British market for each area, and agreeing on a price.

132

The United States also has followed similar policies in limited areas. Ever since the middle 1930's the Congress has passed a series of sugar acts that establish a quota in the United States market for every important sugar-producing area in Latin America, plus the mainland United States, Hawaii, Puerto Rico, and the Philippine Islands. Prices are also established, within certain limits. During World War II the United States and the main coffee-producing countries of Latin America joined to establish a quota system for the United States market, fixing both quantities and prices. More recently, an international coffee agreement involving the principal Latin American and African producers and the United States and some important European consumers, was reached in 1959. It seeks to limit quantities of coffee coming onto the world market to an amount roughly equivalent to world demand.

In the case of minerals and some agricultural raw-material products, the United States policy of stockpiling has had somewhat the same results. Various organs of our government have entered into contracts extending over various years for the purpose of steady purchase of tin, copper, rubber, and other products.

These partial programs give some indication of how a general plan for stabilizing international commodity prices might work. Such an international program has a number of points in its favor. Many industrial countries have recognized the dangers of sharp and rapid changes in demand for and price of agricultural and mineral commodities insofar as their national economies are concerned, and have sought at least to provide floors for the prices of these products in their own national markets. If such a program is valid for a single nation, it is equally valid for the underdeveloped nations and the countries to which they sell the bulk of their products. In many cases stable prices and demand for their principal export products would make it possible for the underdeveloped nations to plan their development without recourse to loans or grants from abroad. If they could plan for a reasonably long period on the basis of reasonably certain knowledge of at least the minimum amout of foreign exchange income they were to get from their raw materials and foodstuffs, they could take steps to put aside a certain percentage of their foreign exchange income for economic development—for the importation of capital equipment needed for growth. Such planning is virtually impossible now in the face of unstable markets and the consequent rapid fluctuations in the amount of foreign exchange income earned from their exports.

A program for international stabilization of raw-material and foodstuff prices would probably necessitate the establishment of some kind of "buffer stocks" for the principal products involved. The buffer-stock organization would be empowered to purchase quantities of these products when the price in the international market fell below an agreed-upon figure. On the other hand, the buffer stocks would be authorized to sell from their pools of products when prices rose above an agreed-upon amount. The purpose would be to maintain prices within certain agreed-upon bounds.

Undoubtedly such a program would present many difficulties. First of all, there would undoubtedly be much negotiation and even wrangling between the producers and the principal consumers of these products as to just what was a "fair" price. Second, a buffer-stock system would probably necessitate some method of fixing quotas for those countries already producing the products involved, opening another field for disputation. Third, the fixing of quotas would have the tendency, unless steps were taken to prevent it, of freezing out of production countries that were seeking to enter the market for the products in the buffer-stock plan. This problem might be dealt with by making a general estimate of consumption possibilities, in the time period immediately ahead, and then setting the quotas somewhat below the estimated demand. This would permit the entry of new countries into the market, or some expansion of the output of already established producing countries.

Another possible objection to such a scheme would be that it would "disrupt international trade." This argument has been frequently made in the past. Of course, one's position on this issue depends upon the angle from which one is viewing the question. The underdeveloped nations feel that there has been a great deal of "disruption" and chaos in the existing system of more or less "free trade" in their products. They feel that by and large the present system is so arranged as to play into the hands of the already developed nations.

Certainly, the objectives of such a scheme not only would be to assure stability of prices but also to assure greater equality of bargaining power for the underdeveloped nations in dealing with the already developed ones. However, if the industrialized countries are really sincere in their professed concern for the development of the underdeveloped nations, this should not be a serious criticism of the scheme.

The establishment of a buffer-stocks scheme would necessitate a certain amount of concession on both sides. The industrialized nations might find themselves paying consistently higher prices than might otherwise be the case over a considerable period of time. However, from time to time the underdeveloped nations might find that they would have to forego the advantages of sudden price rises in their products. For instance, if the coffee buffer stock had the purpose of keeping coffee at, let us say, $0.90 a pound, this might usually aid the producing countries. But there would also be periods in which droughts or other natural catastrophes might tend to push the price above $0.90, at which point the buffer stock would be authorized to sell part of its holdings in the world market, thus depriving the producing nations of the advantages of temporarily higher prices. The underdeveloped countries could not expect the buffer-stock scheme to work out to their long-run advantage if every time temporary conditions forced prices above the agreed-upon price they would seek to withdraw from the scheme. This, indeed, is what happened to the Inter-American Coffee Agreement after World War II.

CONCLUSION

Both an expanded program of economic aid through loans and grants, and a system for stabilizing international prices of the principal raw-material and food commodities, would call for considerably more coordinated effort in economic development than has been evident during the years since World War II. Valuable time has been lost during the decade and a half that has elapsed since the end of the world conflict. The pressure for economic development has been mounting steadily; crises in their programs of growth have developed in one country after another. These crises have engendered a considerable degree of frustration and bitterness in many of the underdeveloped nations, and have contributed notably to world tensions and lack of international understanding. The launching of an imaginative and reasonably daring new program of world-wide economic development would go far to relieving the unrest of a large part of humanity, or at least channeling this unrest in constructive paths.

9

The Entrepreneur, the Manager, and Economic Development

Innovation is at the heart of economic development. Unless there were someone in a society who was willing to try new methods, new machines, new institutional arrangements, the diversification and industrialization of a nation's economy would be impossible. The ones responsible for such innovation we may call "entrepreneurs."

In the older industrialized nations the concept of the entrepreneur has become a common one. The folk heroes of these countries are frequently the bright young men with new ideas who fought until these ideas were accepted, some great new invention was a working reality, and the innovation of the entrepreneur was a success. However, in the underdeveloped countries the entrepreneur is not yet a common phenomenon. Indeed, in the earlier phases of development he is considered an interloper, a disturber of the collective peace. It takes time before there develops a class that has as one of its principal functions that of innovation.

TRADITIONAL SOCIETIES

The underdeveloped nations are generally countries in which tradition rather than innovation is the rule. The economic activities of the people are carried on as prescribed by custom; the relations of one group to another are determined by tradition. Personal loyalties between one person and another, rather than the impersonal forces of the market, are the hallmark not only of economic life but also of politics and society in general.

Thus the relations between the semifeudal landlords of Latin America and their tenants are determined by customs at least as old as the Spanish Conquest of the sixteenth century. The relationships between the members of the characteristic village in India or Pakistan are steeped in tradition, reinforced by religion and superstition. The tribalism of the majority of the native peoples of Africa creates a society rich in custom but largely unacquainted with the monetary values of the market society of industrialized countries.

Tradition-oriented societies are generally nonmarket societies. Production of goods is usually conducted for the satisfaction of the needs of the family or the village. Goods that the local group cannot produce for itself it obtains by barter from neighboring villages, barter that is itself frequently controlled by custom-established rules. The exchange of goods or services for money, when it exists at all, involves only those few goods which cannot be obtained from within the local community itself. It involves relatively few people, and they are often outsiders, who are not bound by the customs and traditions of the society. Thus, in medieval Europe the great traders and moneylenders were the Jews, who were outside the pale of the Christian civilization of the time. The traders and entrepreneurs of much of Africa are Arabs or East Indians. Many of the early traders and industrialists of Latin America were immigrants from Europe or western Asia who were unacquainted with the traditional patterns of the new countries to which they came.

But these outsiders are the exception. Generally, the ideas of production of standardized goods for sale in a general market, instead of for local use; of employment for wages that in turn are used for purchasing needed goods and services; of saving and the accumulation of capital equipment—these are absent from a preindustrial society. Banking institutions and the concept of "negotiable instruments" of "commercial paper"—pieces of paper representing debts or property ownership, such as notes, bonds, stocks, which can be freely bought and sold—are beyond the ken of the majority of the people in such a society.

Of course, this custom-dominated and traditional orientation of society prevailed in western Europe during the Middle Ages, perhaps even down to the Industrial Revolution of the eighteenth century. The evolution from a custom-dominated to a market society in that part of the world spread over a period of many centuries, and even today there are remnants of the traditional society in many of the European nations.

The United States and other former British colonies—Canada, Australia, New Zealand—whose population consists principally of offspring of European immigrants, are probably the only countries that generally have never had this custom-based, traditional type of society. Settled largely by people who ran away from or were forced out of the customary societies of Europe, they found that in the countries of their adoption innovation was necessary in order to survive. Furthermore, these countries were settled by the "mother country" largely for the purpose of supplying it with goods it could not grow or produce for itself. These new countries, therefore, were from the beginning market societies, where goods were produced for sale and where self-sufficient agriculture—the most fecund producer of a static and tradition-oriented society—was never of major importance.

However, even in these former British colonies there are regions that have developed tradition-oriented societies. Parts of the southern part of the United States, as well as much of the French-Canadian province of Quebec, are in this category. In the latter area, in particular, the forces of custom and tradition have actively fought industrialization and a modification of the status quo.

IMPACT OF INDUSTRIAL NATIONS ON TRADITIONAL SOCIETY

Long before the current drive for economic development of the underdeveloped countries got under way, most of the traditional nonmarket societies had been severely disturbed by the impact of the commercial, industrialized societies of western Europe and the United States. As early as the first decade of the nineteenth century, the British economist James Mill wrote about the disastrous effects of the introduction of British machine-made textiles into India upon the native cottage textile industry. Even the natives of many European colonies in Africa had been forced by the imposition of a head tax or a tax on their huts, payable in money, to go out of their villages to earn their tax money by working on European-owned plantations or in the mines.

The search of the already industrialized nations for new sources of raw materials to supply their factories and food to feed their growing populations contributed considerably to undermining the traditional economies and societies of the underdeveloped countries. It introduced thousands of workers to the wage system and a monetary economy in the mines and on the great plantations. It brought with it the introduction of modern means of transportation and stimulated the growth of cities, where the hold of tradition and custom was less strong than in the countryside. It resulted in the establishment of the rudiments of a banking system in many of these nations, and made other far-reaching changes. However, in spite of the changes brought by the foreign firms, the traditional way of life still continued to be followed by the majority of the people in most of the underdeveloped countries.

If the presently underdeveloped nations were to wait for the effects of foreign mining and agricultural enterprises to engender sufficient spirit of enterprise to assure the kind of rapid growth of the economy their leaders and vocal citizens desire, they would be disappointed. As we have indicated elsewhere in this volume, the growth tendencies in the already developed and the newly developing nations are such that the gap between them is tending to get wider rather than narrower, even in spite of the energetic efforts toward development of the governments of the developing countries. In all but a very few countries, if it were not for these efforts, the prospects of the underdeveloped regions ever catching up with the industrialized nations would be all but hopeless. Without some outside stimulation, the "natural" processes of the preindustrial society would not be nearly sufficient to guarantee steady or rapid growth.

INNOVATION AND ECONOMIC DEVELOPMENT

Those seeking to stimulate the drive toward industrialization and economic development find that one of their most difficult problems is to overcome the hold of tradition and to find means for getting the process of innovation started. Once innovation, and not tradition, becomes the general custom of the community, the process of economic growth has overcome one of its most severe handicaps.

The problem is a dual one. On the one hand it is necessary to develop a group within the economy whose role it is to be peculiarly concerned with innovation. On the other hand, it is equally important that the spirit of innovation be to a considerable degree spread throughout the community.

In the countries of western Europe and the United States, which were the first ones to experience modern economic development, the role of innovators has been largely occupied by the private businessman. He it is who has been the principal investor of capital, the principal experimenter with new ideas, new methods of production, new capital equipment, and different ways of getting commodities to the consumer.

However, even in these countries the role of the government as an innovator should not be overlooked. In recent years the impact of an extensive government development program —the Tennessee Valley Authority—was necessary in the southeastern United States before the hold of tradition could be broken there, and the burden of innovation be shifted to the private businessman.

In some countries which could fairly be said to have moved from the "underdeveloped" to the "developed" column before World War II, the government has played a dominant role as the innovating force. This was obviously so in the Soviet Union. However, it was only a little less the case in the Germany of the kaisers and in Japan. In Germany the government heavily subsidized the growth of industry, while in Japan the government itself became the direct innovator, turning industrial operations over to private businessmen only after they had been successfully established.

In the presently underdeveloped countries, it is virtually inevitable that much of the burden of innovation should be borne by the government. It is the only institution able to mobilize all the factors of production—the labor, the capital equipment, the raw materials, the funds—necessary for rapid economic growth. If the underdeveloped nations did not want to see their economies grow very rapidly, they perhaps could afford to wait for the effects of the impact from the already industrialized nations to create a class of private entrepreneurs who would be willing and able to become the innovators. However, there is even some doubt as to whether such a class would within the foreseeable future be in a position to overcome the traditions and customs that are holding back economic development. In any case, the underdeveloped nations do not feel that they have the time to wait for the by no means certain growth of a private entrepreneurial class.

The state is in a position to give a sufficiently great shock to the *status quo* in the custom-dominated nations to overcome traditional inertia. Through planning for development, through active encouragement of industry, by extending protection to it as well as by investing in it, by obtaining the services of entrepreneurs and managers from abroad, it can get the process of development well under way.

The governments of the developing countries also provide the motivation for innovation. Although the desire for private profit, which was the principal motivation in the Anglo-Saxon countries, is too weak to be effective in most of the newly industrialized countries, nationalism does provide a motivation of the necessary power and magnitude. In the name of nationalism these states can rapidly sweep aside traditional barriers that would be impenetrable to a private profit seeker on his own. New methods and the sacrifices often required by innovation can be made legitimate by appeals to national loyalty and pride.

However, in few countries in the non-Communist world does the state carry the full burden of innovation. Foreign firms from the already industrialized countries have a very important role to play. They not only bring in new machinery and means of production; they bring also new ideas about the way firms producing for the market should be organized, about how the market itself should be developed, and about how goods should be presented in the market. Lack of knowledge and naïveté sometimes lead these foreign enterprisers to make mistakes, but on the balance their effect in transforming a tradition-oriented society into a market one is positive.

The author encountered in one of the Latin American countries an almost facetious example of the kind of effect firms from abroad sometimes have. A large United States merchandising company had established a department store in a large Latin American city. It used advertising methods that, for this city, were new and daring, and they were closely studied and even copied by locally owned competitors. Indeed, so closely were they copied that one month when the United States firm ran low on its advertising budget and decided to cut the size of its regular ads in the local press, all the native competitors followed suit, and reduced the size of their advertisements too. They reasoned that if the Yankee firm behaved that way, it must be engaging in some maneuver designed to get more customers and extend its market.

Of course, mere imitation of the operations of foreign firms is not enough to engender a native class of entrepreneurs or innovators. However, in time, such a class does emerge. With experience, the new industrialists, merchants, and other businessmen become more used to trying not only new ways of attracting the consumer but also new methods of turning out their product, of organizing the enterprise, and of dealing with its work force. They discover that innovation is essential to expansion and growth not only of their individual enterprise but also of the economy as a whole.

Thus the government, foreign firms, and native private entrepreneurs all play an important role in breaking the hold of tradition and custom as the principal determinant of economic life. As economic development continues, there emerge groups among the government planners, the foreign companies, and the new classes of industrialists, modern merchants, bankers, and other businessmen, who have among their principal tasks that of innovation.

However, in a highly industrialized society, innovation is not confined to those whose business it is to innovate. Perhaps as much is contributed by the average worker in the shop and factory, by the rank-and-file salesman, by the outside inventor and "idea man," as by the managerial class and the businessman. A worker makes a small modification in his machine, and when this is multiplied by hundreds of thousands or millions of workers the sum total of these changes is highly significant. The individual foreman finds a more efficient way of arranging his machines or of organizing the production

145

line, and for the particular work at hand this may be a fundamental innovation. A salesman discovers a more persuasive way to present his product to potential customers, which serves to amplify the market, at least for that product. The lone inventor—a favorite theme of literature in the industrialized countries (including recently the Soviet Union, with Dmitri Lopatkin, the inventor being the hero of Vladimir Dudintsev's best-selling novel *Not by Bread Alone*)—still is an important cog in the chain of mechanical innovation.

Potentially, the rank-and-file innovator can be as important in the presently developing nations as he is in the already industrialized ones. However, this too takes time. A worker must have familiarity with machinery, and with his own particular machine, before he is likely to come up with suggestions for improving it. A class of "born salesmen" must be developed before merchandising methods will be subject to the piecemeal type of change and improvement we have described above. Large segments of the population must become acquainted with machinery, motors, and gadgets before very many people will become fascinated with the possibilities of invention and the discovery of new ways of doing everyday things.

The wide diversification of the process of innovation in this way goes far to assure that economic growth has become a spiraling and cumulative phenomenon—that is, that it is likely to grow upon itself. Every successful new inventor stimulates others; every salesman who learns a better way to sell a mousetrap encourages others to go and do likewise; every worker who is rewarded in time or money for an improvement on his machine will be an example others will be likely to follow.

TYPES OF INNOVATION

In the first stages of industrialization, the principal emphasis is on innovation through the introduction of new methods of producing goods—that is, by machine production as opposed to hand manufacture. The introduction of the machine is itself the single most important innovation. Subsequently, methods of marketing, methods of organization of the firm, and other problems becoming increasingly important, though never eclipsing the role of changes in the "means of production."

Most of the native industrialists are self-made men. They began as small artisans or merchants, and their businesses have grown through plowing their profits back into the enterprise. They are not trained in the intricacies of "business management," "labor relations," and all the other specialties of the businessman in the more highly developed economies. They have to learn by doing.

Frequently, however, the entrepreneur in the underdeveloped countries—be he a government official or a private businessman—can overcome some of his own deficiencies by getting the aid of foreigners. Hence, in Latin America a disproportionate number of general managers, heads of sales departments, chief engineers, and chiefs of personnel are foreigners. They come from Italy, Germany, Great Britain, and from the United States. They have the skills the owners of the local firms lack, and they are very useful in training a native managerial and entrepreneurial group to take over in the future.

In India the same kind of service has for many decades been rendered by a unique institution—the management firm. British enterprisers set up in business as managers and entrepreneurs and in the beginning offered their services principally to large British companies that wished to do business in India. As Indians became interested in establishing manufacturing industries and other modern firms, but lacked the necessary know-how, these management firms began to secure employment from them. Finally, in recent years, there have been considerable numbers of Indian managerial firms, which have played a key role in the growing industrialization of that country, offering their services to foreign investors, Indian investors, and the government alike.

In most of the countries new industrialists are saved from the effects of their mistakes while learning to be entrepreneurs by the fact that they enjoy a monopoly or near-monopoly position for a considerable period of time. In a country that has had no textile plants, the first person to establish one has a high degree of monopoly if his new industry is protected by high tariffs or other governmental measures. He can afford to make mistakes because he does not have to face competition. However, as the number of firms in the trade increases, the cost of mistakes gets greater, since competitors will be likely to take advantage of them to increase their business at his expense.

One of the dangers in this situation is that the monopolist producer will seek to get the government to save him from the results of his own errors by preventing the introduction of rival firms. We have commented upon this problem in another chapter of this book. However, it is worth while to note here that if competitive firms are prevented from developing, this is likely to stunt further growth of the industries in which it occurs, and will prevent the industrialist from passing from what may be called the first stage of his enterprise to the second stage.

The second stage of development of the firm in the under-developed nations arrives when the entrepreneur becomes aware of the deficiencies of his enterprise, begins to suffer from them, and to become aware of the need for changes. Innovations thereupon tend to change their nature. Instead of all the emphasis being put on mechanical innovation, the introduction of new machinery, and so on, the emphasis begins to shift to matters of organization, labor relations, and merchandising.

This process might be compared to climbing a mountain. The mountaineer makes rapid progress toward the top while the angle of elevation is sharp. But after a while he comes upon a plateau that extends for a considerable distance in front of him, and no further progress in an upward direction is made for some time. The plateau serves to let him catch his breath, repair broken equipment, or shift his load. If he does not do so, he may well find himself unable to continue the upward climb when he again arrives at a steep elevation.

So it is with the industrialist in the underdeveloped country. In the beginning the angle is sharp; he makes great progress "upward"; his market expands rather rapidly; he can sell all that he can produce; and he is too busy learning to make his plant function and establishing a distribution system of some sort to be aware that he is doing both jobs inefficiently. However, at some point he reaches a "plateau" where he seems to cease further rapid expansion, where he becomes acutely aware of high costs, of inefficient sales methods, and knows that some innovations in these spheres are called for. The author has noted such a development in a number of Latin American countries, and it would seem to be a logical phase in any country's process of industrialization.

When the industrialization "plateau" has been reached, new

talents of innovation are called for. The entrepreneur must eliminate wasteful and time-consuming methods of business organization, perhaps departmentalizing his firm to a higher degree, and developing specialists in various phases of the enterprise, instead of jacks-of-all-trades who are used wherever the need seems greatest. More care must be taken in accounting, and in obtaining the best and cheapest raw materials. A more systematic method must be developed for grooming talented young men in the organization for the jobs in the higher echelons. New outlets for his product may have to be sought, and the nature and quantity of the sales appeal may have to be changed.

Finally, more attention will probably have to be paid to the problem of relations with the workers. Better systems of communications from top to bottom and back up to the top of the firm will have to be developed. Wage systems may have to be reorganized to stimulate greater output from the worker, while assuring him a sizable part of the returns from this greater output. It may also be advisable for the firm to try to divest itself of some of the paternalistic responsibilities for the daily life of the worker that it had to assume in the first phase of the life of the industry.

A developing nation as a whole tends to reach this kind of "industrialization plateau" as much as does an individual businessman. This was demonstrated clearly in Puerto Rico in the middle 1950's, when the planners of the island became convinced that further industrialization and development of the island were being retarded significantly by the fact that no attention had been paid during the first burst of economic growth to the problem of distribution. Although many more goods were now available and being bought by the average Puerto Rican, whose income had almost doubled in the previous fifteen years, these goods were still being sold through the old preindustrial channels of distribution.

The government, which has played a particularly important role in the process of innovation in Puerto Rico, therefore undertook to aid the transformation of the distribution system. It succeeded in getting several firms from the United States to establish chains of supermarkets in the principal metropolitan centers of the island. At the same time it helped financially the development of the consumers' cooperative movement, which also developed a supermarket chain. Goods could thus be bought more economically, more quickly, and in a cleaner and more attractive way by the consumers. At the same time producers had better organized and more reliable channels through which to get their goods to market.

Thus the entrepreneur or innovator is the key figure in the process of industrialization and economic growth. It is his job to break down the limitations tradition and custom impose on economic development in most of the underdeveloped countries. In today's world the state will almost inevitably play a large role in sponsoring and encouraging innovation, particularly in the early phases of development, though both foreign and domestic private entrepreneurs will also be of key importance in most countries. Finally, the process of innovation is a complicated and diversified one. Its generalization is an assurance of the continuance of spontaneous growth of the economy.

10

Labor Problems in Economic Development

One of the most difficult problems of economic development is the creation of a modern labor force, with the training and capacity necessary for an advanced economy, and accustomed to the discipline of factory life. People in the already advanced countries more or less take such a labor force for granted, but in fact much time, energy, and resources are necessary to bring it into existence in an underdeveloped nation.

SOCIAL TRANSFORMATION AND ECONOMIC DEVELOPMENT

In most of the developing countries, workers who enter industry are not merely changing their occupation; they are

153

adopting a wholly different way of life. They are moving from one kind of civilization into an economy, a society, or a culture that is entirely different from anything to which they have been accustomed.

A few examples of the nature of the shift will illustrate our point. In Latin America the industrial worker is likely to be recruited from the agricultural laboring force. In most countries of the area the agricultural worker is likely to be a squatter or a share tenant, who receives little or no money income but who works for the landowner in return for the right to use a small piece of land to grow the meager necessities for himself and his family. He has had little or no experience with modern machinery; he has had little or no practice in handling money; he has generally worked at his own pace and, within limits, when and how he wanted to. He has depended completely on his landowner-employer for help in whatever emergencies life might present to him. He has been illiterate, and has had little incentive to be anything else, since the gulf between him and his employer has been so wide that it has seldom if ever occurred to him that it could be crossed.

The peasants of the Middle Eastern countries, who make up the new industrial labor force of those areas, perhaps have an even greater transition when they move from their accustomed occupations into urban industry. They come from a life— not infrequently a migratory life—that has not changed greatly since the days of the Prophet. They too are illiterate, know little or nothing of machinery, and in many cases have not even had a fixed abode.

Finally, the Negro peasant of many parts of Africa comes from a culture of witch doctors, from a grazing economy, or one of subsistence agriculture of virtually the Stone Age level of sophistication. However, he may in some cases have an advantage over his Latin American or Middle Eastern brother in that he may have had some experience with work in the mining industry, to which he had allowed himself to be attached in order to earn enough money to pay his hut tax.

The creation of an adequate modern industrial labor force, therefore, involves a vast clash of cultures, and an adaptation by the new industrial worker to a kind of life of which, perhaps, he has not even dreamed. Although the spread of industrialism to outlying parts of the world has amply disproved any assertions that only certain races or peoples are "capable" of participating in an industrial society, there is no doubt that much time and energy are needed in order to develop an industrial working class in a newly advancing country in the quickest and least painful way, and with the least possible disruption of the fabric of society.

THE PROBLEMS OF LITERACY AND TRAINING

One of the major aspects of the problem is that of literacy. People living in industrialized countries find it hard to understand how important and fundamental is the ability to read and write, which seems to them so simple. Although illiterates can certainly become industrial workers, those who do are hampered in their work in an infinite variety of ways. An illiterate worker cannot read the simplest of signs or instructions telling him that he should not smoke or that he should take care of his machine in a certain way. He finds it much harder to learn what his rights and his duties on his job are. He finds it impossible, perhaps, to do certain necessary things such as reading blueprints or reading notices about changes of routine in the plant. It becomes all but impossible for employers to engage in safety campaigns, to maintain channels of contact with their employees through bulletin boards, house organs, and other such instrumentalities.

Literacy, then, is one of the great cornerstones of an efficiently operating modern industrial society. The lack of it is one of the principal handicaps a nation that is entering the phase of economic development and industrialization must overcome. Economic growth, therefore, must be accompanied by a rapid development of the basic educational system. Industrialization does not mean just the construction of factories, mines, and transport systems, but also the building of a school system that can feed into this new economic life a working class capable of putting the new capital equipment to the best and most efficient use.

However, basic education—literacy or the three R's—is not enough. Recruits to the new working class must be provided with the skills they need to operate the machines and implements with which they must work. Residents of the highly industrialized countries, again, find it hard to conceive of how completely unused to mechanical gadgets new industrial workers in the developing countries are likely to be. In the United States, western Europe, and other countries in which agricultural machinery has come into general use, the farm boy is early acquainted with the equipment on his father's farm, with how it operates and how it is repaired. Furthermore, he is likely to know many of the intricacies of an automobile, a radio, a clock, or in these days even a television set. His whole youthful life is impregnated with ideas of machinery and of the complex technological society in which he is brought up.

In contrast, the new worker coming out of the countryside of Latin America, the deserts of the Middle East, the villages of India, or the bush of Africa has virtually no such knowledge. He has perhaps seen airplanes fly overhead, or has seen an automobile bump along the local roadways—and may even have ridden in one—but he has no practical experience with them. A hoe, a forked stick, a wooden or iron-tipped plow is the height of his mechanical sophistication. Unacquainted personally with autos or clocks or radios, he has never tinkered with them. Unable to read or write, he has never read about them. He comes to his new industrial employment innocent of all practical knowledge of the kind of machinery with which he must work.

The author of the present book had a graphic experience with the phenomenon we are discussing. A young West African man of his acquaintance, already in his late twenties, came to visit immediately after arriving from Africa. It was necessary to explain to him how a toilet worked, and for several days the visitor did not take a bath because he did not know how to make the bathtub and shower function. The television set was a constant source of amazement, and even a ride on the train was a fascinating new experience for him. Yet his education was superior to that of the vast majority of the new industrial workers in the developing countries, and his sophistication was vastly greater than that of the average peasant who comes to work in urban industries.

The burden of equipping the new industrial workers with the skills of a modern technological society is one that is usually borne both by the employer and by the educational authorities. Employers attempt to attack the problem in many different ways. Probably most general is the simple process of putting a raw, untrained worker alongside a more experienced companion to learn by example. However, this procedure not only wastes the time of the already trained workers but also means that the new employee does not have the expert kind of training he probably needs.

Many employers in underdeveloped countries have their own training programs, putting aside a part of their plant and some of their machinery for this purpose. In some countries, notably Brazil, the employers carry out extensive training programs through the medium of their associations and confederations.

However, a large part of the work of developing a trained and skilled work force must inevitably fall upon the government. Education for work in industry must begin very young, and generally the establishment of adequate schools for this purpose involves fundamental changes in the educational system as it has existed heretofore. Before the process of economic development and industrialization gets started, the schools of most underdeveloped nations are generally designed to train a social and cultural elite. They lay great emphasis on literacy and general cultural subjects—a perhaps ridiculous example is that of teaching Latin to many of the secondary students in East Africa. There is therefore a great need to put more emphasis on vocational education, technical training, and the manual arts, without losing sight of the general cultural objectives of any education.

HEALTH PROBLEMS

Of equal importance to the education and technical training of the new industrial worker is the problem of his health. Generally speaking, the agricultural worker or peasant of the economically less advanced countries tends to suffer from undernourishment as well as from endemic diseases. This is true in spite of the immense progress that has been made in public health services in these parts of the world, particularly since World War II.

A sick worker is not generally a good worker. He loses a large amount of time from his job, and cannot give his full energies to it even when he is physically present. Furthermore, his family's health is of almost as much importance from an economic point of view as is his own. A worker distracted by a great deal of sickness at home is not likely to be able to devote his full attention to his job, even if he himself is in good health.

Hence, industrial and similar employers in the underdeveloped nations are likely to find that they must come to grips with the health problems of the worker and of his family. Employers frequently find it necessary to have a doctor on the premises, or at least to have his services readily available for their workers and for the workers' families. In the case of larger firms, the employer will frequently build a clinic or a small hospital.

It is also notable that social-security systems of the underdeveloped nations tend to lay a great deal of stress on the provision of health insurance for the worker and often for his family as well. Illness is the greatest single economic hazard the new industrial worker is likely to face, and the social-security systems are adapted to this fact. Not only is workmen's compensation—hospitalization and other aid for workers injured or made ill on the job—almost always the first type of social security to be established; general health insurance is also usually the second.

PROBLEMS OF INCENTIVE

The background of the new industrial worker in the underdeveloped countries usually presents his employer with serious psychological problems as well as physical problems to deal with. One of these is lack of incentive. In the milieu from which the new industrial worker has come the gap between himself and his landlord or employer has been so wide that he has hardly considered the possibility of crossing it. Furthermore, since harder work on his part generally has seemed only to benefit his employer, he has seldom felt any great desire to do any more work on his landlord's land than that which is absolutely necessary.

One of the most important labor problems in economic development, therefore, is that of convincing the worker that it is possible for him to move ahead, that he will have something to gain from more conscientious and painstaking work. Time is necessary before this realization comes to the worker. He must become aware of the fact that he has moved from a society that has only two steps on its ladder into one in which the gradations between those at the very top and those at the bottom are increasingly numerous—and that he, or at least his children, if given the chance, can rise up at least one or two of these steps.

In part, the lack of incentive for the new industrial worker arises from the limited needs to which he had been accustomed before coming to the city. The possibility of changing his situation had been so remote that his needs had come to be limited to the barest minimum of food, clothing, and shelter. Merely coming to the city to work in industry does not immediately widen his horizons. Hence, there is more than a little sense in the old story that a new worker is likely to labor only so long as he needs to do so in order to purchase the things to which he has traditionally been accustomed. If that takes six days' labor a week, he will, perforce, work for six days. But if it takes only three or four days, he will work only three or four. However, when he has acquired new wants or new ambitions, for himself or his family, this initial tendency toward absenteeism is likely to disappear.

However, once the worker has become convinced that he can improve his status and his economic situation, another problem is presented. In his new-found desire to move up the social—or economic—ladder, he may acquire too simplistic a view as to how this can be achieved. There is no doubt that this is one factor in explaining the somewhat turbulent relations existing between the workers and their employers in many of the underdeveloped nations. It is also a partial explanation for the followings demagogues often have in these nations.

LACK OF FAMILIARITY WITH MONEY INCOME

Allied to the problem of arousing incentives is the problem of the new worker's inexperience with money income. Most newly recruited industrial workers in the underdeveloped economies come from some sort of subsistence agriculture. They have grown most of their own food and have made most of the other things they need. They have handled very small amounts of money.

Once they get to the city, however, the workers find that they get what at first appears to them to be very large amounts of money. It takes some time before they make the complementary discovery that they are expected to pay for all their expenses out of these sums. There is a tendency on the part of the new worker to spend all his income within a short time after receiving it.

This tendency is reinforced by a number of factors. Most nonindustrial societies are characterized by a species of "conspicuous consumption" even on the part of the poor. Certain celebrations and fiestas call for the expenditure of large amounts of money on entertainment and merrymaking. Such events, indeed, are the principal entertainment of people in these societies, and are deeply ingrained in their culture. The trait is not one that is easily cast off by workers moving out of the countryside to work in urban industry.

Furthermore, in some countries, at least, there is a tendency toward debauchery of the rural worker. This has deep cultural roots, also, but there is no doubt that in some instances it is encouraged by rural employers as a method of maintaining control over the workers. Excessive drunkenness is one of the most frequent vices of this type. This, too, a worker tends to take with him when he migrates to the city. He is likely to spend a large part of his income on getting drunk, and is often likely to miss work owing to the same cause.

In Mexico and Chile this problem is so common that Monday, the first working day of the week, has come to be referred to jokingly as "San Lunes." Santo Domingo, or Sunday, is a day of rest, and for those who drink too heavily over the weekend, Lunes, or Monday, is likely to be the same, so it is also dubbed as if, like Sunday, it were named after a saint.

EMPLOYER PATERNALISM

This problem of lack of familiarity with money income has been a principal cause of a phenomenon that one frequently finds in labor-management relations in the underdeveloped nations—paternalism. One finds that employers tend to provide for many more of the needs of their workers, and to interfere much more in the private lives of their employees than is the case in the economically more advanced countries. This tendency is largely owing to the desire of the employer to build up a healthy, educated, and trained labor force as rapidly as possible.

Employer paternalism touches on many aspects of the worker's life. Employers frequently provide housing for some or all of their workers. Such housing is provided not only because no other housing is available in the community but also because this is a very useful device for arousing incentive in workers and even for educating them to a new way of life. If the employer does not provide housing for all his employees, he can select those to whom he does make homes available on the basis of their attendance at work, their skill, or other criteria. Frequently employers seek to oversee the way in which the workers use the housing they are granted, carrying on a campaign to teach the workers to live in a more cleanly and responsible way.

Educational facilities, both for the workers and their off-spring, often are also provided for the workers by their employers. Medical help and hospitalization are likewise part of the programs of many paternalistic employers. So are company stores, where the workers can buy their principal staples at cost, or sometimes at less than cost. These stores help the worker to become more adept at living upon his money income, and help compensate the workers for the fact that money wages in most underdeveloped countries are still, for the most part, distressingly low. Sometimes these low-prices stores are organized as cooperatives with the workers having a part in their management.

Employers in the newly developing countries often find themselves called upon to help tide their workers over financial crises. In view of the low level of wages, and the workers' unfamiliarity with money income, few workers in the underdeveloped countries are likely to be able to save very much. As a result, when some particular crisis arises the worker turns to the employer to borrow money to tide him over. In Latin America, at least, this writer has found that virtually every industrial employer has some kind of system for making wage advances to his workers when the need arises.

Sometimes the employers are consulted by the workers on problems about which workers in the more highly developed countries would not consider approaching their employers. Family troubles and psychological problems of one kind or another are likely to be brought to the attention of the employers. As a result, many employers in the underdeveloped nations have found it worth while to have social workers as regular members of their staffs. These workers, with some training in psychology, are able to listen to the workers' private problems and to give advice and sometimes help in resolving them. The social workers are also often given supervision of such things as housing programs, and the advancing of money by the employer to the workers.

One interesting aspect of employer paternalism in many of the underdeveloped countries is the fact that it has not been opposed, generally, by the trade unions. The workers' organizations have rather tended to look upon employer housing, education, health, and other projects as "conquests" by the workers, and have sought to maintain and extend them rather than abolish them. This attitude of the worker is in sharp contrast to the situation in the already highly developed countries.

In many countries the friendly attitude of the workers toward employer paternalism has its roots in the cultural and social background of the workers themselves. Frequently the new industrial worker comes from an agricultural background where he was more or less completely dependent upon his employer for meeting all his big and little crises. Moving to the city and going to work in a factory or some other industrial enterprise, the worker tends to regard his new employer in more or less the same light as he did his old one. He tends to look to him whenever he has a problem he cannot solve. He goes to him to get advice, to borrow money, to get help when he or his family are sick, when he wants to send his children to school, even when he is having trouble with his wife or his children. The worker therefore finds it quite natural that the employers should set up means and methods to resolve these and many other problems.

These paternalistic activities of the employers add greatly to the cost of labor in the underdeveloped countries. Although money wages are generally very low in the less advanced countries, the indirect expenses involved in paternalistic programs may make the total labor costs quite high.

Sooner or later it is likely that the employers will want to shed many of their paternalistic responsibilities. In some of the Latin American countries this tendency is already visible. Employers are tending to sell the workers the houses in which they live; they are trying to raise prices in the company stores to those prevailing in the market place, and ultimately to get rid of the store altogether. They are seeking to get the state to assume the burdens of education and medical care. However, it is likely that for some time to come employer paternalism will be a feature of labor relations in the underdeveloped countries.

LABOR DISCIPLINE

All the problems we have discussed so far are closely connected with the problem of labor discipline. This is one of the most difficult aspects of labor relations in the developing countries.

The discipline needed to make a factory run efficiently is of quite a different sort from the discipline to which a worker has been accustomed before coming to work in industry. Even in countries characterized by semifeudal types of land-holding the agricultural worker is usually more or less free to work in his own time and at his own speed. So long as he gets his assigned tasks accomplished, he is not likely to be subject to the minute supervision of anyone else. Seldom does he have to work steadily eight hours a day and six days a week.

However, when the worker comes to the factory he is presented with a situation that calls for a much more concentrated type of work than he has been accustomed to in the countryside. There are definite work hours, and there are rules that must be obeyed if the factory is to function efficiently. It is frequently very difficult for the worker to accustom himself to this type of operation.

As a result, absenteeism is very high. Workers arrive late on their jobs, and they may miss a day's work or more a week. An increase in wages will in many cases only make the situation worse. Labor turnover also tends to be high. Workers will become dissatisfied with the situation in the plant where they are employed, and will shift from one place of employment to another. Finally, much generalized discontent arises from the worker's unwillingness to submit to ordinary factory discipline.

In some countries that have gone through the economic development process it has been possible to adapt old customs and old loyalties to the new industrial situation, and thus overcome the problems of factory discipline. For instance, during the industrialization of Japan, workers for the factories were often recruited from rural areas by village elders to whom the villagers felt ties of loyalty and obedience. If they were sent to work in a factory by the elders, the workers felt that they owed them the obligation of doing the job well, and were therefore willing to subject themselves to whatever terms and conditions were proposed by the factory owners.

In other countries, kinds of forced labor have been used, particularly in mining enterprises. In South Africa and some of the other African countries this type of labor recruiting has been particularly notorious. Workers have been brought from long distances, kept as virtual prisoners in compounds, and have been always available for work.

In most countries the Japanese situation has not existed, and the South African system has not been regarded as just. Therefore, the task of breaking workers into factory discipline has been much more difficult. Without either the workers' sense of moral obligation or methods of compulsion, employers have had patiently to educate the workers to what is needed, through offering inducements to good workers and threatening punishment to bad ones.

Sometimes it takes a whole generation before this problem has really been resolved. The author has been told by various employers in the underdeveloped countries that they are anxious to employ sons and daughters of workers already in their employ, because these young people are accustomed to factory life. They know their rights and obligations before they go to work, and they have never had the experience of the kind of rural employment that "spoiled" their parents for the factory regimen. Furthermore, these young workers have heard enough shop talk in their homes to be acquainted in some detail with the kind of work they will be expected to do.

CONCLUSION

The development of a stable, productive, and disciplined work force is thus one of the principal problems of economic growth. It creates difficulties and situations that are quite unfamiliar to residents of the older industrial countries. Upon its successful accomplishment depends, to a very large degree, the fate of the development program of the economically less advanced nations.

11

Trade Unionism, Social Legislation, and Economic Development

A characteristic of today's underdeveloped countries is the existence in virtually all of them of more or less powerful trade-union movements and of extensive social legislation. In this respect currently developing nations differ fundamentally from those countries that industrialized during the eighteenth and nineteenth centuries. This situation creates kinds of problems with which those earlier industrial nations had little experience.

In Great Britain, the original modern industrial country, the first serious legal restrictions on the employer's ability to exploit his workers came only fifty to seventy-five years after the beginning of the Industrial Revolution. It was not until a century after the beginning of the factory system, in the 1850's, that trade unionism gained a strong foothold. In the case of the United States, although the process of industrialization had got under way before the Civil War, it was not until the 1930's that unionization became common in the basic mass-production industries. Extensive social legislation also came into vogue in the United States only in the 1930's.

However, the currently developing nations are attempting to industrialize in a world in which trade unionism is already well established and in which there are constant pressures from inside and outside their borders for them to enact advanced social legislation that their economies are in many cases hard put to sustain. Thus there are serious limitations placed on the exploitation of the workers, which in all developing nations has been the principal source, or at least one of the principal sources, of the accumulation of capital.*

REASONS FOR TRADE UNIONISM

There are several reasons why trade unionism and social laws are so common in the underdeveloped nations today. Three of these reasons are of particular importance: the propagation of these ideas from the already developed nations; nationalism and the desire to "keep up with the international Joneses"; and the existence of political democracy.

By the time the countries of Asia, Africa, and Latin America began economic development in earnest, trade unionism and radical political ideas often associated with it had a strong hold in the already developed countries. Great Britain and the other countries of western Europe, as well as the United

* By "exploitation" we mean quite simply a situation in which workers newly brought into modern industry from more traditional parts of the economy receive only a small share of the increase in their own productivity arising from this change in economic activity.

States, had strong and wealthy labor union organizations. Political parties associated with them had representatives in the parliaments, and in some cases they controlled governments. There had come into existence even before the First World War an international labor group, the International Federation of Trade Unions, which, though largely European, aspired to become truly world-wide.

A great deal of literature was written about the labor movement and its problems. Intellectuals and better educated workers in the underdeveloped nations had read much of this literature, including programs and proclamations of the European and United States labor organizations. Not inconsiderable numbers of people from colonial areas and from Latin America as well had had more or less personal contact with organized labor in the industrialized countries.

The people of the underdeveloped countries were also aware of political developments in Europe and North America. The Russian Revolution had a profound effect on the economically less advanced nations, especially because of the insistence of the Bolshevik government that it was presiding over a "workers' state." Later events such as the New Deal in the United States and the advent of the Labor party to power in Great Britain also had their impact on the people, particularly the workers and intellectuals, of the underdeveloped nations.

As a result of the spread of unionism and the ideas associated with it, and of political developments in Europe and the United States, the concept of working-class solidarity and organization for mutual defense spread into the economically less developed parts of the world. In some cases these ideas were absorbed before there was really much of a working class to organize.

A second reason for the spread of trade unionism into the

economically less advanced nations was the rise of nationalism. This had two effects. In the first place, nationalism generated considerable pressure within the underdeveloped nations to allow trade unionism and to pass social legislation as a means of maintaining national prestige. The author remembers a conversation with a leading Latin American statesman who was responsible for the beginnings of extensive labor legislation and legal recognition of organized labor, in which he stressed that his country had been inspired to pass its early laws for the protection of labor as a result of its membership in the International Labor Organization, and its desire to fulfill its obligations to that group.

The growth of nationalism had another effect favorable to the organization of the workers. Many of the enterprises in the underdeveloped countries that employed the largest numbers of workers—the mines, railroad systems, large agricultural enterprises—were owned by foreign firms. Thus the struggles of the workers of these firms took on a patriotic coloration they would not otherwise have possessed. The workers were not only trying to get justice from their employers; they were also trying to assert the rights of citizens of the underdeveloped countries against the foreign interloper. As a result of this, the early labor organizations in these foreign-owned enterprises were frequently able to arouse general support among the populace that they could not otherwise have obtained.

Finally, in those nations emerging from colonial status the labor movement has drawn much strength from its close association with the movement for national independence. Led largely by nationalist intellectuals, the trade unions became a major means for rallying support behind the anticolonial movement. In this process they acquired a strength and a popularity among nonworking-class groups in the community

172

that they would not have acquired if theirs had been a purely economic struggle.

The existence of a degree of political democracy in most of the underdeveloped countries also favored the early development of trade unionism and social legislation there. This also was in contrast to the situation in the older industrial countries. In Great Britain the Industrial Revolution occurred at a time when the suffrage was limited to the aristocracy and the masses had not yet entered into politics. The same thing was true of Germany. In the case of the United States, there existed universal manhood suffrage during the industrialization period, but until recent decades the farmers were of such political importance that they were able to block the aspirations for labor and social legislation of the still weak trade-union movement.

However, in the presently underdeveloped nations, the process of economic growth and industrialization began in an era in which universal suffrage is already achieved. As a result, politicians there early came to realize that a group of organized workers, if properly mobilized, could be a powerful force in political affairs. In countries where governments were changed by the ballot, they might well be a decisive element at the polls; in cases where change of government came about by more violent methods, the organized workers could also be very useful in helping politicians with whom they were friendly and hurting those toward whom they were hostile —through the general strike and other coercive methods. As a result, many politicians not only encouraged labor to organize, and passed social legislation for their benefit, but also sought to impose certain controls over the unions, to keep them from being used against themselves.

As a result of all these circumstances, virtually all the underdeveloped nations have trade-union movements. In some of these countries, such as Argentina, for instance, where large numbers of European immigrants brought trade unionism and radical political ideas with them, the labor movement dates from the last couple of decades of the nineteenth century when railroaders and artisan groups began to establish their organizations. At the other extreme are countries such as Morocco and Algeria, where trade unionism among the native Arabic-speaking population virtually did not exist until the 1950's.

POLITICAL NATURE OF ORGANIZED LABOR

Trade unionism in the underdeveloped countries has certain characteristics that tend to distinguish it from the same phenomenon in the already developed nations. The first of these is the particularly heavy emphasis the trade unions of the less advanced nations usually place on politics. In most of these countries the central labor organizations (equivalents of the AFL-CIO) and most of their constituent unions are under the control of one political party or the other. There is a tendency for the trade-union movement to be a tool of the politicians, instead of the trade unions trying to use one or another political party for their own purposes.

The reasons for this phenomenon are somewhat complex, but not difficult to understand. First of all, in most of the underdeveloped nations the unions are financially weak. Their members receive very low wages, and therefore cannot pay very high dues. Furthermore, in most of the underdeveloped countries the workers are not accustomed to paying dues regularly to unions or to any other group. As a result, the trade unions often do not get from their membership the funds they need to conduct their operations, and as a result they have to look outside for help. As a rule, they turn either to the government or to a political party.

In the second place, intellectuals—and hence politicians—often play a leading role in starting trade-union movements in the underdeveloped nations. (It might be noted that the same thing was true in the early days in Great Britain, the United States, and Germany.) It is frequently the intellectuals who are filled with ideas about the injustice of the way in which the workers are treated and who frequently set out to try to do something about it by organizing the workers so that they can help themselves.

In the countries that have recently emerged from colonial rule it has been the intellectuals who have taken the lead in the struggle for national independence. As one means of mustering mass support, many of the nationalist intellectuals turned to the labor movement, and it was only after independence had been achieved that divergences frequently began to appear between some of the independence leaders and the organized workers.

In independent countries and colonies alike, the trade unions needed support from powerful political interests. Not only did they need protection in cases of sharp conflict with their employers; they also sought to achieve the passage of legislation favoring and protecting the workers. As a result, it is natural that the labor movement should seek some sort of arrangement with some of the existing parties, or help bring into existence new political organizations. However, in view of their financial weakness, it is not surprising that the workers' groups tended at first to be the junior partners in any such alliances.

For their part, government officials and political leaders frequently had their own reasons for seeking influence among the new trade unions. Some of them sought it for purely opportunistic political reasons; other did so because they believed in a particular political program that was favorable to the workers.

The net result of this has been that the trade unions in the underdeveloped nations have been very closely associated with politics. A few cases will be sufficient to indicate this: In India there are three major central labor organizations, each affiliated with one of the three major political parties, the Congress party, the Socialists, and the Communists. In Tunisia the two trade-union groups are affiliated with the governing Neo-Destour party and the Communist party. In Chile virtually every trade union in the country is under the influence of the Socialists, Communists, Radicals, or Christian Democrats. In Ghana the unions are under the leadership of members of the Convention People's party, the party of Prime Minister Nkrumah. In Kenya the Trade Union Congress is the basis of the Negro nationalist movement. In Mexico almost all union groups are affiliated with the government's Revolutionary Institutional party.

There are visible certain tendencies toward a lessening of political influence within the unions in some of the underdeveloped countries. It seems likely that as the workers become somewhat better off and can more easily afford to pay dues, and as the unions are able to achieve some form of the checkoff (whereby the employers deduct the dues from the workers' wages and pay them directly to the union), the unions will be able to play a more independent role vis-à-vis the parties and the governments of the underdeveloped nations.

This tendency toward independence will in all likelihood also involve certain changes in the structure of the trade-union movements. When the industrial sector of the economy is small, and industries are concentrated in a small number of cities and towns, the most logical form of organization is that based on geography. That is, the workers of a particular trade or industry are organized in a given city or region, and then all the unions of that region are brought together in a local central labor organization. National central labor bodies (comparable, let us say, with the AFL-CIO or the British Trades Union Congress) are then created on the basis of these local central labor groups.

However, with the growth of industrialization and the development of really national industries, there is a tendency for the unions also to become national. When there are metal-working firms scattered throughout a country, for instance, it is logical for the metalworkers of the whole nation to tend to form a national metalworkers' union. This is all the more true when a metal plant in one part of the country is in direct competition with one in another part of the country—in a word, when the market for their products is a truly national one. With the establishment of national trade or industrial unions, the tendency grows to establish the central labor organization on the basis of these national unions.

The whole emphasis of the trade-union movement then shifts. As long as the basis of the organization of the labor movement is a geographical one, with the power resting in local central labor bodies, there is a greater temptation for the organization to be principally political, since political activities are basically geographical. Campaigns are fought on a geographical basis, and local politicians build up their strength locally. However, once the center of gravity of the labor movement shifts to the national trade or industrial union, the tendency is for the interest of the unions to shift from concentration on political matters to concern for economic problems. A national union, negotiating contracts with the employers on a nation-wide basis, or supervising the negotiation of local contracts, will perforce have to spend most of its time on these problems. Although it may still pay some attention to political matters, if only in self-defense, its principal concern is likely to be the negotiation and administration of collective agreements.

GOVERNMENT CONTROL OF UNIONS

As a direct result of the close connection between the trade-union movement and politics in the developing nations, the labor movements of most of those countries are rather more closely controlled by the government than is true in western Europe and the United States. This is true in the Latin American countries, most of which have extensive labor codes, as well as in the former British colonies, where British colonial trade-union regulations have been kept by independent governments.

Such controls extend to a number of aspects of the internal life of the unions. They include more or less close supervision over the finances of the workers' organizations, as well as over their electoral processes and their political activities. There is also considerable control by the government over the actual process of collective bargaining, ranging from compulsory mediation and conciliation (intervention by the government in an attempt to get the parties to reach a voluntary agreement) to compulsory arbitration—leaving the final decision in cases of deadlocked disputes up to the government.

In a number of countries recently emerged from colonial status, there has been a tendency for government control over the unions to increase after the achievement of independence. This arises in considerable degree from a conflict in interest between the new governments and the labor movement. The governments put main stress on rapid economic development, whereas the unions are anxious to see to it that this development doesn't take place at the expense of their members.

SOCIAL LEGISLATION

Closely allied to the rise of trade unionism in the underdeveloped countries has been the extension of social legislation. This falls into four general categories: laws controlling the unions, employers' associations, and collective bargaining, which we have already noted; what is usually called factory legislation; statutes dealing with wages; and social security.

Factory legislation involves various kinds of rules for the protection of the worker. The limitation of hours of work is one example. Most of the underdeveloped countries—like the more industrialized ones—have limited working hours to eight per day, save in exceptional circumstances, and to forty-eight per week. These laws, by and large, are well enforced.

Other types of factory legislation include laws for the safety of workers, such as those requiring guards and controls on dangerous machinery, the provision of gloves and special equipment for certain kinds of jobs, and the provision of emergency exits. They include laws providing special consideration for women and minors, such as the widespread practice in Latin America whereby employers are required to provide nurseries for very young children, and time during the workday for the mother to nurse her infant. Many countries also have laws providing for a paid-vacation period for the worker, which may be put in the same general classification.

Many underdeveloped countries have enacted special legislation dealing with wages and salaries. Most general are laws providing for minimum wages. Usually countries that have minimum-wage laws provide that the minimums shall be different in different parts of the country, or shall be different in different industries. They almost always provide for some kind of periodical revision and adjustment of the minimums. Other kinds of laws dealing with wages include those that call for equal pay for equal work, which demand payment of wages in money and not in any kind of tokens, and those which specify that wages must be paid at stated periodic intervals.

Sometimes the benefits that labor legislation attempts to extend to the workers are excessive, so much so that they have an effect opposite to that intended. A typical case of this is the famous "tenure" law of Brazil. According to this law, an employer cannot dismiss a worker after ten years of employment without paying an indemnity which in some cases amounts to as much as $50,000—and can only do that with the approval of a labor court and the worker's union.

The effect of this is to have many employers dismiss workers long before they have reached the ten-year mark. The labor courts have insisted that if a worker is dismissed after nine years this is an attempt by the employer to violate the law. So, to be safe, many employers get rid of any worker who has been in their employ for seven to seven and a half years.

This situation works to the detriment of both the workers and the employers. Many good workers are dismissed merely because their employer fears that they may acquire tenure, and thereafter prove not to be good workers any longer, leaving the employer with the alternative either of bearing with them or paying them an excessively large indemnity. On the other hand, many employers lose out by dismissing workers who are very good at their jobs and whom they really need. Such an attempt to give aid to the workers thus turns out, in fact, to do them considerable damage.

SOCIAL SECURITY

Finally, there is social-security legislation. An observer from one of the economically more advanced nations will be struck at how extensive social security is in the underdeveloped countries. Few of these nations are without some kind of social security. For reasons we have mentioned elsewhere, workmen's compensation—provisions for workers who have been injured or who got sick on the job—is usually the first type of social security to be established, and health insurance is the second. However, very frequently there is also provision for some kind of old-age retirement, special provision for widows and orphans, special provision for working mothers, and so on. Even family allowances, whereby a worker is paid so much each month from social-security funds for each child dependent upon him, are not uncommon.

About the only kind of social-security measure that has not been widely adopted is unemployment insurance. This can probably be explained by the fact that unemployment arising from economic depression has not been a major issue during the 1940's and 1950's when most of the social-security legislation of the underdeveloped nations was being adopted. An attempt to deal with more long-run kinds of unemployment problems—those arising from overpopulation or hidden unemployment, for instance—would be too great a task even for the optimists who draw up the social-security legislation of the underdeveloped nations to undertake.

Some social-security systems in the economically less advanced nations go to abusive extremes. That of Chile is a case in point. The system there works in such a fashion that an employee can be a member of more than one of the country's various social-security funds. At the same time, he can retire after a certain number of years of employment, regardless of his age. This results, in a number of cases, in a worker "retiring" under one system and drawing a pension while he continues to work in his employment covered by the other system until he has been engaged long enough to draw a pension there too. One social-security fund, that of the railroaders, allows a worker to retire, under certain circumstances, after only ten years of employment. Although such situations might be tolerable in an immensely wealthy economy, that of Chile is not one of these, and the burden is too great. The excessively costly Chilean social-security system adds very appreciably to that country's inflationary pressure.

Another type of abuse is that of the government's failure to contribute its share of the cost of social security. Most systems are established on a basis that takes into account the payment into it by three parties—the employer, the worker, and the government. When one party fails to pay its allotted share, the whole system is undermined. This is notoriously the case in Brazil, for instance, where in 1956 the government owed the equivalent of approximately $293,000,000 to the country's social security funds.

The net effect of trade unionism and social legislation in the underdeveloped nations is mixed. However, on the balance these things probably act as a drawback to development, making it more costly, and slowing down the rate of capital accumulation.

LABOR AND INFLATION

The existence of trade unions with more or less strength makes it more difficult to pass on the costs of economic development to the workers. It makes it harder to keep down the money wage of the worker, so that the owners of new industries—be they private firms or the state—can take the lion's share. It puts the workers in a better position to demand that a larger part of the increases in production be given to those who are employed in this production. Hence, it makes it more difficult than it would otherwise be to plow back into the creation of more capital goods the returns from the growth of output coming from the process of industrialization and economic growth.

In actual practice, this problem is at least partially overcome by the process of inflation that plagues many of the underdeveloped nations. Although unions succeed in pushing up money wages periodically, these increases are quickly offset by increases in prices. The profits of the owners of industry—whether private firms or the state—thus remain high, and a considerable part of them are plowed back into further development.

Social legislation also adds to inflationary pressure. This is particularly true of social security. The costs of social-security programs to the employer in some of the underdeveloped countries are almost unbelievable to residents of the already industrialized nations. In some of the Latin American countries social-security amounts to one-third of the basic wage cost, while other social legislation sometimes involves further costs amounting to another third of the wage bill. These costs are generally passed on to the consumer in the form of higher prices.

There is as yet little indication, insofar as the author can ascertain, that union pressure and social legislation are having in the underdeveloped nations the effect that the late Sumner Slichter credited them with in the industrialized nations. That is, there seems to be relatively little evidence that constant pressure of the unions and government agencies for higher wages is tending to make the employers seek through greater mechanization to reduce the labor cost per unit of output. In those countries in which employers are becoming conscious of the need to reduce labor costs, this is a relatively new development. In most nations, however, the answer of the owners of industry to the problem of greater costs is merely to raise prices.

LABOR AND ECONOMIC GROWTH

However, the effects of trade unionism and social legislation in the developing countries are not entirely detrimental to economic growth. First of all, the efforts of the unions certainly do have the effect of maintaining the market for the goods produced by the new industries that are being created. To the degree that the unions keep up the workers' wages, they are maintaining the workers' purchasing power, their ability to take off the market the goods they produce. It should be noted, though, that at the present moment the insufficiency of capital for future development is a greater problem than that of inadequately expanding purchasing power.

In the second place, the funds collected by the social-security systems are usually direct aids to investment. They are generally borrowed by the governments concerned for purposes of investment in capital accumulation—frequently in housing construction, but often in other types of capital development as well.

In general, it can probably be said that the advantages of trade unionism and social legislation in the underdeveloped countries are greater in terms of psychological and social values than in an economic sense. The greatest single gain from trade unionism, in the author's opinion, is the fact that the worker becomes a citizen of industry through it. Where a trade union of some strength exists, the workers are not treated as virtual slaves or as mere "costs of production," as was true in Great Britain during the Industrial Revolution, and in the Soviet Union during the first phase of its industrialization. Rather, the workers can, through their representatives, speak as equals or near equals with the owners and managers of their enterprises. They are given a dignity and a respectability that cannot be measured in terms of statistics or money but that are of tremendous value for the present and future development of these countries.

In the second place, in spite of inflation and other methods used to avoid the impact of the unions and social legislation, it is undoubtedly true that in most of the presently developing countries the worst kinds of exploitation, which characterized the industrialization process in Great Britain and Russia, are being avoided. The workday is kept within reasonable limits; some of the worst hazards facing the worker, such as sickness and accident, are provided for; women are not forced to do work to which they are not physically adapted; children are not forced to work on a large scale in industry; the tempo of work is kept relatively moderate.

These are all certainly gains from a human point of view. They make the industrialization of the presently underdeveloped countries a much less horrible and horrifying process than was the same event in many of the earlier industrial countries. However, whether they are conscious of it or not, the governments and peoples of the underdeveloped countries are choosing between a more humane type of industrialization and rapidity of development. They have decided for the former. There are few who would quarrel with this decision —the author certainly would not do so.

12

The Stake of Democracy in the Economic Development of the Underdeveloped Countries

The fate of democracy in the underdeveloped countries, and probably in the more advanced industrial nations as well, depends in large part on the ability of the less advanced countries to make their economies grow rapidly and steadily. This fact is too little realized, unfortunately, in the democratic industrial countries, though the Soviet Union would seem to be fully aware of it. The ability of the democratic nations to understand the importance of economic development to their own future is limited by fears concerning the possible consequences of the economic growth of the presently unindustrialized parts of the world.

The fears that economic development engenders in the more advanced democratic countries are many, but they can be summed up under three headings. First, there is fear of the economic consequences of development, fear that the newly industrializing countries may become formidable competitors with the older industrial nations. In the second place, there is fear of the politico-military effects of the growth of new industrial powers of first rank. Finally, there is a largely unspoken but nonetheless potent fear based on race prejudice and the "peril" involved in seeing the colored two-thirds of humanity rise in importance, wealth, and power.

There is of course an element of truth and justification in the fears of the people of the industrialized nations concerning the economic effects of economic growth and industrialization in the underdeveloped nations. It is undoubtedly true that with the progress of industrialization in the underdeveloped countries, those nations will produce for themselves many of the products—particularly the light consumers' goods—which they formerly purchased in the industrial nations of western Europe and North America. The fate of the British textile industry is sufficient evidence of this. Britain formerly sold a large part of its textile production to India and other colonial territories. When, after World War I, India was given the right to raise tariff barriers against the importation of British goods, and behind those walls began to develop its own textile-manufacturing industry on a large scale, the British textile industry suffered a crisis from which it has not yet emerged. The United States textile industry has experienced the same kind of phenomenon, though on a lesser scale, as the result of the development of textile industries in the Latin American countries.

However, this is only one side of the picture—and the less important side at that. Although some industries in the earlier industrial countries may suffer from the development of the less advanced nations, other, and more important, industries in the already developed countries will stand to gain. The nature of the goods bought by the developing nations in the already industrialized ones will change, but the total amount of goods bought is likely greatly to increase.

Economic development of the currently underdeveloped nations will result in vast increases in the purchasing power of the people of the developing countries. Whereas only a small percentage of the population of most of the countries of Asia, Africa, and Latin America now receive sufficient money income to buy more than a few dollars' worth of goods in the market, economic development will change this situation. The expansion of agriculture, the growth of industry, and the development of service trades in the presently less advanced nations will result in rapidly growing numbers of people earning wages, salaries, and profits that they will spend on consumers' goods. The higher their incomes go, the more diversified will these people's purchases become.

As a result of this process, hundreds of millions of people who now buy little or nothing will be in the market for an increasingly wide range of goods. Many of the goods that they will wish to purchase will come from abroad. Only the most fortunately endowed of the presently underdeveloped countries will be likely to be able to supply most of the increased needs of their consumers, especially for heavy or "durable" goods. The desire of the presently underdeveloped nations to buy consumers' goods from abroad, therefore, will increase. Automobiles, radio and television sets, refrigerators, and all the other "gadgets" that characterize modern industrial civilization will be in demand by people who never dreamed of possessing them before the advent of industrialization.

The entry of 400,000,000 Indians, nearly 100,000,000 Indonesians, nearly 200,000,000 Latin Americans, and 100,000,000 Africans into the market for the first time on a large scale cannot help having favorable effects on the demand in those countries for manufactured goods and other products made or grown in the already highly industrial countries.

However, increase in the demand for consumers' goods—particularly heavy consumers' goods—will not be the only result of the growth of the presently underdeveloped nations' economies. Even more important during the first stages of development will be the demand for producers' goods—for machines, turbines, electric motors, power plants, railroad rolling stock, trucks, bulldozers, and a host of other kinds of capital goods. Although some of the underdeveloped countries will be able to produce some of these goods for themselves, most of them will have to acquire these abroad.

One significant fact about both heavy consumers' goods and capital equipment is worthy of note. The country that first sells such goods to the people of the underdeveloped country will be likely to have a considerable advantage over its competitors. When it comes time to buy spare parts or replacements, it will be natural for the user in the underdeveloped nations to turn to the source from which he made his original purchase. Thus patterns of trade will be established, trade names will become well known in the underdeveloped country, and the first sellers will have an inside track on their competitors from their own country and from other countries.

All these facts indicate that the economic development of the underdeveloped nations will rebound economically to the advantage of the highly industrialized countries. Although some light consumers'-goods industries in the earlier industrial countries may suffer, other industries will find additional sales opportunities, and the total increase in purchasing power of the underdeveloped nation will result in a large increase in the total amount the country is likely to want to purchase abroad.

ECONOMIC DEVELOPMENT AND INTERNATIONAL TRADE

The likelihood of this development is demonstrated by present-day international trade patterns. The best customers of the United States are not the economically most backward nations. Most of them are countries that are highly industrialized or on the way to industrialization. Great Britain has for long been the United States' best customer; Canada lags only slightly behind. Our trade with most of the important European industrial powers is greater than our trade with all but a very few of the underdeveloped nations.

The fact is that a country with a diversified economy, which brings its whole population into the market and which has reached the stage at which every new step of economic growth generates other steps, will inevitably be a much larger purchaser of goods from abroad than an underdeveloped country most of whose people draw a miserable existence from subsistence agriculture. The incomes of the people of the first type of country are many times higher; their desires for goods are more diverse, their tastes more varied. Thus, even though a country may turn out its basic needs for a product, there may well be a demand for some of that same product from abroad to satisfy a slightly different taste.

The United States is a good example of what we mean. The United States produces wines, but there are many in the country who prefer French or Chilean or Spanish wines, and can afford to buy them. The United States produces textiles of all kinds, but there are people who prefer to buy British woolens, and do so. The United States leads in the manufacture of automobiles, but there are those who prefer European cars. The United States grows tobacco, but the taste of our consumers demands that it be mixed with tobaccos of Turkey and Greece.

Economic development of the underdeveloped countries may be a partial answer to one of the basic problems of the economies of the already industrialized nations: the problem of the business cycle. Growing sales of consumers' goods and capital equipment to the developing nations will serve to keep large numbers of workers in the already industrialized countries employed. Furthermore, the planned nature of the development programs of many of the underdeveloped nations will mean that those nations' demands for capital equipment will be relatively steady. They will not fluctuate as violently as the demand for similar products within the highly industrialized nations themselves, with their lesser emphasis on planned development and their greater reliance on the "natural" forces of supply and demand to keep up production. This fact should contribute to greater stability in the highly developed nations.

ECONOMIC DEVELOPMENT AND THE
BALANCE OF POWER

The largely unfounded fear of the economic consequences in the industrialized nations of the development of the unindustrialized ones is frequently reinforced by apprehension concerning the political and military consequences of economic development. There is fear that the growth of the economies of some of the presently underdeveloped countries may make these nations politically much more important, and militarily a "menace." The implicit feeling is that the growth of the political and military power of the underdeveloped nations will result in a relative reduction in the influence of the present "Great Powers," notably the United States.

It is certainly true that if India or Brazil, for instance, takes its place among the world's major industrial countries, as either may well do within the next generation, its voice will carry much more weight in international affairs. It will be able to maintain, and probably will maintain, larger, more powerful, and more modern military establishments than either now possesses.

However, it is also true that both India and Brazil—as well as most of the other underdeveloped nations—are at the present time democracies or are striving to become democracies. They will probably remain democracies if they are able to develop their economies quickly enough to give their people hope of better standards of living and a fuller life. Only if their people become too frustrated, only if they find that too many of the things after which they aspire are unobtainable in the foreseeable future, will these countries and others like them turn from democracy to some other way of life. The best guarantee that these stronger voices at international conference tables will be voices for democracy is that they make sufficient progress in developing their economies and raising their peoples' standards of living so that the masses of these nations continue to have hope and continue to be able to take pride in their countries' achievements. Frustration and hopelessness will militate against a firm basis for democracy. The rapid and steady progress of economic development of the nations on this side of the Iron and Bamboo curtains is the surest means of assuring that these countries will not become totalitarian and that their growing power and influence will be used on the side of democracy.

Not all the new industrial powers that will appear in the decades to come will be part of the so-called Western Alliance. Indeed, few of them may be. With their preoccupation with the problems of economic development, they will tend to want to form a bloc apart from either the Communist sphere or the sphere of the older industrial powers of the West. However, if they become more powerful, politically and economically, they will constitute a considerable deterrent to possible adventurism by the rulers of the Communist bloc. The Communist rulers will not only have to take into consideration the possible reactions of the Western Powers—whom they consider enemies in any case—but also those of the new industrializing Neutral Powers, whose stand may well be decisive in any showdown.

Finally, the rise of new Great Powers from among the presently underdeveloped countries may have another kind of positive effect on international politics. One of the major problems of the years since World War II has been that there have been in fact only two Great Powers. They have been engaged for more than a decade and a half in parrying each other. Whatever one of them has done, the other has done something else to counter. All international questions have been considered almost exclusively from the point of view of their effects on the power position of these two Great Powers. Virtually anything proposed by one was automatically vetoed by the other. As a result, there has been a kind of stalemate on all international questions of major importance.

The rise of new Great Powers will tend to alter this situation. It will give more room for maneuver in international politics. It will make it possible for the new Great Powers to act as buffers to the older ones, to bring forth ideas and suggestions on a variety of problems that will not necessarily be rejected out of hand by either the Soviet Union or the United States. One cannot help thinking that the climate of international relations will be healthier when the world is no longer divided into two great warring camps.

ECONOMIC DEVELOPMENT AND RACISM

The third kind of fear in the older industrial nations concerning the growth of the underdeveloped countries is less frequently expressed and more insidious than those we have already discussed. With the exception of Japan, the presently developed nations are all European or have populations predominantly of European stock. There is unquestionably fear in these countries of the rise of powerful colored nations.

This kind of fear is unreasoning and irrational, but perhaps there is little argument that can prevail against it. However, those who feel this way should undoubtedly pause to take certain facts into consideration. The first fact is that two-thirds or more of the world's population is colored. The white one-third has dominated the colored two-thirds for several centuries, but it can do so no longer. The colored nations are in their vast majority now independent, sovereign powers; and those that are not are soon likely to become so. This historical trend cannot be reversed.

Furthermore, the several centuries of white rule over the rest of the world has left among the colored peoples bitter resentments and deep-seated anger. The touchiness of the new countries of Asia and Africa and the older ones of Latin America concerning the problem of the remaining colonial territories is ample evidence of this fact. The only way in which the countries peopled by Europeans and their offspring can overcome these resentments is to acquiesce in the growth of the countries encompassing the other two-thirds of the earth—and, going further than mere acquiescence, to extend a helping hand in aiding them to grow, economically, politically, and in every other way.

There are highly embarrassing and explosive aspects to this problem. The white peoples of the earth occupy areas that are relatively lightly populated—with the exception of a few of the European countries. In contrast, many of the under-developed countries suffer from excessively large popula-tions. If these nations are not able to develop their resources and to demonstrate rather quickly that it is possible to raise their peoples' standards of living, the cry is likely to be raised sooner or later for the opening up of the predominantly "white" areas to the people of the overcrowded portions of the earth. (Ironically enough, the Soviet Union, not any of the countries of the so-called West, may well be the first predominantly white nation to be faced with such a demand.) The only way in which such a wholesale migration of peoples can be headed off before it begins is by the rapid development of the economies and standards of living of the presently underdeveloped nations.

All the fears of the economically advanced nations concerning the development of the rest of the world should pale before the key fact of the situation: the underdeveloped nations are going to develop whether the present industrial countries like it or not. As we have indicated throughout this book, economic development is now virtually an article of faith in most of Asia, Africa, and Latin America.

ECONOMIC DEVELOPMENT AND
THE COLD WAR

If these countries can get help in their economic development from the countries of western Europe and North America, they will, for the most part, welcome it. If they cannot get it from there, they will seek it—and are seeking it—elsewhere. If they cannot get aid from any industrialized country, they will continue to try to develop their economies anyway. The process will be much more painful for the developing countries in this last case than it might otherwise be. However, that will be no deterrent. It will merely mean that the development process will take a little longer and that it will breed insurmountable resentment against those more fortunate nations that might have helped them but did not do so.

The Communist countries are doing their utmost to stimulate such resentment. Furthermore, they are presenting to the gaze of the underdeveloped nations a glowing picture of the success the Soviet Union has had and China is having in developing their economies by totalitarian methods. There is little doubt that the rapid conversion of Soviet Russia from a backward agricultural nation into the world's second largest industrial country has a tremendous power of attraction in the underdeveloped nations. One of the most dramatic features of present-day Asia is the race for development between democratic India and Communist China. The leaders of both countries are well aware of its significance, and the Indians are constantly comparing their efforts to those of their huge neighbor.

Although the leaders of the underdeveloped nations have some conception of the tremendous cost Soviet Russia had to pay to achieve its rapid economic development—cost in terms of low standards of living and of political tyranny—many of their less worldly-wise countrymen are not so aware of this. They see the tremendous economic achievement, but do not notice the blacker side of the picture. Hence Soviet Russia stands as a constant example to them of what a nation that is really intent on economic development can achieve by its own efforts. So far, the leaders of the underdeveloped countries have been able generally to keep the blinder admirers of the Soviet in check. How long they will continue to be able to do so is a matter of conjecture.

For their own best interests, the countries of western Europe and North America should begin to extend aid on a hitherto unprecedented scale to the underdeveloped nations. They stand to gain economically and politically from so doing. If they do not follow such a policy, they are placing in jeopardy their own national existence. They are also imperiling the future of the democratic way of life that is the greatest contribution the West Europeans and their offspring have made to human civilization.

One may argue that the western countries, and particularly the United States, have already extended a considerable amount of help to the developing countries. This may be so, when one looks only at the total figures in cold print. But the fact is that even at its height, such aid has seldom if ever amounted to 1 per cent of the national income of the Western world, or even of that of the United States.

These countries have been willing year after year to spend as much as 20 per cent to 25 per cent of their national incomes on arming for self-defense in the immediate future, but they have not been willing to spend a very small portion of that amount on the only thing that can in the long run assure the triumph of the ideas and ideals for which they claim to stand. Military defense is unquestionably of key importance in holding off the threat of military aggression from the Communist countries, and the author, for one, would not want to see it lessened at this time, though he might question the judgment of some aspect of "defense" planning, particularly with regard to giving antiquated arms to broken-down dictators in various parts of the world, whose only purpose in acquiring these arms is to oppress their own people, not to defend their nations and the non-Communist world in general against the military threat from the Communist countries.

However, all the military preparations that western Europe and the United States can make will not be sufficient if, through "oversight" on our part, we allow the underdeveloped parts of the world to turn toward Communism. This will certainly occur if these nations' aspirations for economic development become severely thwarted, or if the pressures built up by the process of diverting resources from an already very low per capita income become too great.

There are those who will reply that "charity should begin at home" and that rather than spending untold billions of dollars on the development of the economically underdeveloped nations these funds should be spent on helping the growth of those parts of the industrialized nations that still are relatively backward. There is of course much merit in such expenditures within the industrialized nations, but these need not exclude overseas development. Furthermore, aid to the underdeveloped areas has an urgency and a long-range importance for the whole future of the world that projects within the already advanced countries do not usually have. Finally, it is highly doubtful whether, in the United States at least, such domestic programs are feasible in any case for some time to come. The prejudices against "Socialism" and "big government," and the vested interests of those who for one reason or another do not want regional development programs, public housing, large-scale school construction, and so on, are still too great.

There will be difficulties in any large-scale program for aid by the industrialized countries to the economic development of the less advanced nations. We have discussed many of them in this volume. There will be need for adequate planning of general economic development as well as of specific projects, so as to avoid wasteful use of resources that, after all, are limited. It will perhaps be difficult to recruit sufficient trained technical personnel from the already industrialized nations to engage in the technical-assistance aspects of a program such as we are suggesting. It will be difficult also to obtain sufficient trained personnel to run large projects once they have been established. However, none of these difficulties is insurmountable.

INTERNATIONAL COOPERATION AND ECONOMIC DEVELOPMENT

One way of overcoming many of these problems, as well as others that may arise in the process of such a program, is by the greatest possible degree of cooperation among all parties concerned. To avoid duplication of effort, this cooperation must not only be between those from a single industrial country that is extending aid and the country receiving it, but should also include the utmost feasible cooperation among the countries of western Europe and the United States that engage in large-scale economic aid programs. Finally, insofar as possible, there should be a more general cooperative effort through the technical and economic development agencies of the United Nations.

Various figures have from time to time been suggested as to the amount that might be spent each year by the United States on such a program of aid to the underdeveloped countries. Some economists have suggested an expenditure of three to five billion dollars a year; Walter Reuther, in a somewhat more heady mood, suggested a program of ten to fifteen billion.

The author is not prepared to suggest any figure. However, it is clear that the approximately one billion which the United States has been spending in general economic aid programs and the few hundred million more it has been making available through the Export-Import Bank and the International Bank for Reconstruction and Development are inadequate.

Recent history has provided us with a technique whereby the extent of such an economic aid program might well be determined. At the inception of the Marshall Plan, the countries that were to receive aid drew up among themselves a suggested program for United States help. The United States government itself appointed a committee to go over the "bill" from the European countries, and to bring in its own report. On the basis of these two suggestions, the United States Congress accepted a general sum of some $19,000,000,000 for the Marshall Plan total.

In the present instance a somewhat similar method might be used. The underdeveloped countries might be invited to get together among themselves, or as regional groups, and draw up a detailed program for development over a period of perhaps ten years, taking into account their own internal resources, what aid they might be able to give one another, and what they would like to receive from the industrial nations. For their part, the countries of western Europe, plus the United States and Canada, and perhaps Japan, might meet, using the report of the underdeveloped countries as their working paper, and draw up suggestions concerning how much they would be willing and able to advance. Their computations should take into account the way in which they wished to make funds and technical assistance available—whether through their individual governments, through some new joint organization, or through the various organs of the United Nations. On the basis of the recommendations of this conference, proposals could be submitted to the legislatures of the various industrialized nations.*

Such a new approach to the problem of economic aid would serve to arouse the imagination of peoples both in the underdeveloped nations and in the industrial ones. It would give notice to the peoples of the underdeveloped countries that the more advanced nations were seriously concerned with their problems. It would also serve to set the limits within which foreign aid to economic development could be expected, and give the underdeveloped nations a basis upon which to establish

* It is interesting to note that the Kennedy administration has been moving in the direction of an approach such as we suggest here since early 1961.

their own planning programs. It might avoid the making of such mistakes as that made by the Indian planners when they overestimated the amount of foreign capital that would be available for carrying out their Second Five-Year Plan.

There are certain precautions that should be taken with this or any other program for aid to the underdeveloped nations. First of all, if such a program is to be successful and is not to engender more hostility than good will, it should not be tied to the West's system of alliances or the West's defense program against the Soviet Union. Rightly or wrongly, most of the underdeveloped nations do not want to become directly involved in the dispute with the Soviet Union. Although they are ideologically democratic, they do not want to have military treaty ties with either side.

As we have indicated earlier, the important thing from the point of view of the democratic nations of western Europe and North America is that the underdeveloped countries remain democratic and that they at least remain neutral. More than this the Western world cannot ask. Indeed, the Western Alliance nations cannot use their promise of aid to try to prevent the underdeveloped nations from accepting such aid as might be offered by the Soviet bloc. If they are going to remain neutral, as they wish to do, some of the underdeveloped nations may feel that they must also accept aid if it is offered by the other side. However, a program of aid such as we have suggested would put the Soviet Union in a position of having to "put up or shut up" on the question of economic aid to underdeveloped countries. It would end the rather ridiculous situation in which the best way for a country to get aid from the West is to accept it from the East.

Furthermore, the countries of the West should always keep in mind the fact that there are underdeveloped nations on the other side of the Iron and Bamboo curtains, and they should stand ready to include these nations in their general aid program if and when one of these nations indicates sufficient independence of Moscow or Peiping to request help from the West.

Finally, the Western world, and the United States in particular, should not use a large-scale economic program to try to force the people of the underdeveloped countries to accept the economic ideology that is most to the liking of the industrialized nations. Probably a cooperative program such as we have suggested would reduce the likelihood of such pressure to a minimum, since there is by no means unanimous agreement among the Western nations concerning economic ideology. But in any case, the Western nations should bear in mind that the principle of noninterference by the state in economic affairs, which is preached (though not always practiced) so ardently by the United States, is not widely espoused in the underdeveloped nations.

For reasons of necessity in most cases, rather than for reasons of ideology, the state is undoubtedly destined to play a very large role in the economic growth of virtually all the underdeveloped nations, as we have indicated from time to time throughout this book. It would be unwise and self-defeating to make an extended program of economic aid the occasion for delivering missionary lectures or stern rebukes concerning the virtues of leaving the economy solely in the hands of "free enterprise." Knowing citizens of the underdeveloped countries will probably be aware that this principle is not adhered to in the United States, but in any case they will certainly not pay much heed to such strictures, and will not thank the United States for fortuitous interference in the economic institutions of their countries.

The Western world is faced with the prospects of "too little and too late." Economic aid to the underdeveloped nations from the industrialized ones has certainly so far been too little. It remains to be seen whether a really adequate program will be too late. There is no doubt that time is running out. The programs of economic growth that the underdeveloped nations are determined to carry through are causing increasing strains on their economic, social, and political structures. One after another these countries are faced with serious institutional crises. In most of them, the traditions of modern democracy are new, and are not as yet deeply rooted. Increasingly, leaders of these nations are asking themselves whether they will have to sacrifice their democratic institutions in order to achieve the rapid material development they seek.

CONCLUSION

The West will have its last chance within the next few years to keep the underdeveloped nations from taking the totalitarian road to economic development that seems at first glance to have wrought such wonders in the Soviet Union and that the Chinese Communists keep telling them is also bringing such rapid economic progress in the world's most populous country. The leaders of most of the underdeveloped nations want to obtain economic development through democratic procedures. If they get sufficient aid from the great industrial nations in lightening the burden of economic development, they will in all likelihood be able to do so. If they do not, they well may be forced to turn to totalitarian methods, or be driven from office by those who are willing to use totalitarian methods. It is for the West to decide.

Bibliographical Note

A great deal has been written during the last decade or so about the problems of economic development. In the present note we wish merely to indicate some of the most important books that have appeared on the subject, with particular attention to those that might be of interest to the noneconomist.

Perhaps the most thorough study of the problems of economic growth to appear has been Benjamin Higgins' *Economic Development: Principles, Problems, and Policies*, published by W. W. Norton & Company in 1959. This is notable not only for the author's own discussion of various aspects of the problem but also for his concise exposition of what most of the important economists who have written about it have said concerning economic development.

A much earlier book is the work of the Australian economist Colin Clark entitled *The Conditions of Economic Progress*, first published by The Macmillan Company in 1940, but which has gone through several later editions. This was a pioneer in the field, and remains one of the most substantial studies of the whole problem.

Several other general studies of economic development are of interest. These include *The Theory of Economic Growth* (published by Richard Irwin, 1955), written by W. A. Lewis, a West Indian who was for many years Professor of Economics at the University of Manchester, England, and served for a time as economic adviser to the government of Ghana. Also, Henry H. Villard's *Economic Development* (Rinehart, 1959), which has some interesting observations on the relationships between economic growth in the Soviet Union and non-Communist countries, is worthy of mention. Gunnar Myrdal's *Rich Lands and Poor* (Harper's, 1957) puts special emphasis on the tendency of the already developed countries' economies to grow more rapidly than those of the underdeveloped nations, thus increasing the disparity between them.

Some writers have been particularly concerned with specific aspects of the problem. These include the Norwegian economist Ragnar Nurkse, in his *Problems of Capital Formation in Underdeveloped Countries* (Oxford University Press, 1953), and Albert Hirschman in his *The Strategy of Economic Development* (Yale University Press, 1958). Similarly, the Harvard Professor W. W. Rostow is particularly concerned in his *The Stages of Economic Development* with trying to develop a generalized pattern of growth from what he calls "the take-off" through the "drive to maturity" to "the age of high mass-consumption," into which all developing nations can be fitted. Finally, P. T. Bauer, in his little book *Economic*

Analysis and Policy in Underdeveloped Countries, pays special attention to the importance of the opening up of mining and plantation agricultural enterprises as a means of getting the process of economic development under way. Robert Aronson and John P. Windmuller, in *Labor Management and Economic Growth*, which they edited in 1954 (Cornell University Press), concentrate on labor-management relations in the developing economies. Similar emphasis is found in *Industrialism and Industrial Man* by Clark Kerr, John Dunlop, Charles Myers, and Frederick Harbison.

Some of the economists who have written on this subject have dealt with it in much more abstract theoretical terms than have most of those whom we have already cited. One of the first to do so was the late Joseph Schumpeter in his *The Theory of Economic Development*, which first appeared in German in 1911 and was published in English translation by Harvard University Press in 1955. Also more theoretical in approach are Harvey Leibenstein's *Economic Backwardness and Economic Growth* (John Wiley, 1957) and Kenneth Kurihara's *The Keynesian Theory of Economic Development* (Columbia University Press, 1959).

In addition to these general studies of the economic development problem, there have appeared a number of studies of the growth problems of specific countries. Outstanding is a series of books published by the International Bank for Reconstruction and Development. These are the result of study missions the bank has sent to various underdeveloped countries from time to time to aid them in planning their economic growth and to suggest fields in which the bank might give loan assistance. The Latin American countries of Colombia, Chile, Cuba, Guatemala, Mexico, and Nicaragua, as well as Jordan, Ceylon, and Turkey in Asia, and Ghana, Nigeria, and Tanganyika in Africa, are among the nations which have been thus surveyed and about which there are interesting books in print.

Numerous other books on the growth problems of specific countries have appeared. Two of these will suffice for our purposes. One is a study, *Costa Rica*, edited by Stacy May and others, published by the Twentieth Century Fund in 1952. Another is William Stead's *Fomento—The Economic Development of Puerto Rico*, published by the National Planning Association in 1958.

The subject of economic development has so far merely been grazed. However, the works we have noted here serve to high-light its growing importance and the increasing fascination the problems of economic growth have for students of all the social sciences, but in particular for the economists.

Index

Absenteeism, 161–162, 166
Agrarian reform, 67, 70–75, 78
Agriculture: dominance of in underdeveloped countries, 9; and population expansion, 26; in economic planning, 56, 57; in Chilean planning, 59; in Ghana, 60; in India, 61–62; in Puerto Rico, 66, 67; in economic development, 69–84; extension service, 79; government investment in, 98; expansion of, 189
Alexander, R. S., xiii
Alexander, Mrs. Robert J. (Joan), xiv
Argentina: economic planning in, 49; landownership system and politics in, 73; professional classes as investors in, 90–91;

sources of industrial capital in, 91; foreign pressures on, 108; railway system in, 110
Armaments, 123, 199
Artisans, 91

Balance of power, 193–194
Balanced economy, 37–40; *see also* Unbalanced economy
Banking, traditional system of, 98; *see also* Central banks; Development banks; Loans
Bauxite, 61
Bolivia, 18, 19 (*table*), 74, 79, 83
Brazil: coffee, 19 (*table*); rubber export, 21; natural resources in, 24; landownership system in, 71; sources of industrial capital in, 90–91; foreign pressures on, 108; foreign aid to,

Brazil (*continued*)
130; social security system in, 182
British West Indies, 132
Buffer stocks, 134–136
Building supplies, 38–39
Burma, 19 (*table*), 25, 74–75, 81

Canada, 53
Capital equipment, 85–87, 123–124, 190
Capital for economic development, 85–102
Capital goods, 9, 43
Carey, Mathew, 35
Carman, Mrs. J. B., xiii
Central banks, 95, 97–98, 99–100
Ceylon, 80
Chile: copper production, 19 (*table*); nitrates export, 22; shoemaking industry, 39; steel industry in, 40–41; foreign exchange control, 47; economic planning, 58–60; agrarian reform, 75; sources of capital in, 90–91; foreign pressures on, 108; trade unionism in, 176; social security system in, 182
Chilean Development Corporation, 49, 58, 60, 100
China, Communist, 53
Cocoa, 19 (*table*), 132
Cocoa Marketing Board, 132
Coffee, 19 (*table*), 22, 133
Cold war, 197–200
Colombia, 25, 74
Colonization, agricultural, 82–84
Commerce, 57
Commodities, international price stabilization, 133
Communications, 60

Communist bloc, 53
Community development, 62
Comparative Advantage, Law of, 31–35
Conspicuous consumption, 72, 88, 161–162
Construction material, 38–39
Consumers' goods: importation by underdeveloped countries, 38; and protectionism, 41; in Indian planning, 63–64; effect of agricultural development on, 77; and dollar shortage, 123–124; competition in, 188
Copper, 19 (*table*)
Costa Rica, 21
Cottage industry, 63–64
Credit, agricultural, 80–81
Cuba, 74, 108
Currency stabilization, 126
Customs, *see* Traditional society

Deficit financing, 95–96
Democracy, political, ix–xi, 14, 173, 187–205
Depression, Great, 22–33
Developed countries: gap between underdeveloped countries and, 51, 53–54; investment in developing countries, 103–117; technological changes within, 112; *see also* Industrial countries
Development banks, 97–98, 100–101
Disarmament, 131–132
Dollar shortage, 123–125, 126–127
Dominican Republic, 108
Dudintsev, Vladimir, 146
Dunne, Finley Peter, quoted, 2